MOTORCYCLING

A PRACTICAL GUIDE

- COMPULSORY BASIC TRAINING
- THE MOTORCYCLE TEST
- ADVANCED RIDING TECHNIQUES

SARAH RUSSON, TOM DUNNE AND BRUCE HARRISON

KOGAN
PAGE

First published 2000

Kogan Page Limited
120 Pentonville Road
London
N1 9JN
UK

Kogan Page Limited
163 Central Avenue, Suite 2
Dover
NH 03820
USA

© Sarah Russon, Tom Dunne and Bruce Harrison, 2000

Artist: Dave Eaton

British Library Cataloguing in Publication Data

A CIP record for this book is available from the British Library.

ISBN 0 7494 2820 1

Typeset by Saxon Graphics Ltd, Derby
Printed and bound in Great Britain by Thanet Press Ltd, Margate

CONTENTS

ACKNOWLEDGEMENTS

The authors and contributors wish to thank those who assisted us with the compilation of this book, particularly family, friends and colleagues, including:

Paul Russon – husband, friend, colleague and once trainee! Thanks for all your support and encouragement, without which this book would never have been started.

John Wilmot (MBE) – friend and colleague. We will be always grateful for your advice during the drafting stage. Your knowledge and experience is invaluable.

Gary Moore – friend and colleague, for always having the time to proof read and assist with editing.

Caitlin Sharrod – friend and guinea pig! Thanks for all your time and help during the early stages. Without your support, I'm sure writer's block would have set in.

We would also like to thank the many experts in the field who have provided us with essential technical information, including:

Paul Britton and Ian Molyneux from Motorcycle Accessories Leicester, for providing us with technical information on helmets and clothing.

Tim, Manager, Motorcycle 2000 Leicester Honda Dealer – for allowing us to take photographs of various machines.

Driving Standards Agency Publications – for providing us with specimen documents.

Mr Andrew Eeles, HMSO – for granting copyright permission, collating all the specimen documents and sending them to us.

Dave Eaton, illustrator – for doing an excellent job in a short space of time. I'm still not sure how you managed to interpret our ideas from a few scribbles!

Louise Cameron, Publishing Manager, Kogan Page – thanks for your commitment during the final stages and for turning the whole project around.

A word of thanks to all the trainees whom we have taught over the years, for it has been said 'Much I have learned from my masters, more from my colleagues, and from my students most of all'.

Our final and biggest thanks goes to Honda UK Ltd, for sponsoring the book and providing material to enhance the overall finished appearance. Without such support, it would have been impossible to produce such a highly illustrated book.

INTRODUCTION

Motorcycling attracts all types of people from all walks of life. Due to a succession of changes during the 1990s, motorcycling has become a fun and accessible pastime.

Safety and training have always been major issues influencing the popularity of the motorcycle. However, thanks to changes in motorcycle design, the law and an increase in motorcycle sales during recent years, motorcycle training has become more widely available and has played a significant role in reducing the number of accidents, particularly those involving the young and inexperienced.

This book has been compiled to aid everyone to become better, safer and happier motorcyclists. Whether just starting out or an experienced rider, this book can be referred to time and time again. Covering many topics, from the law, clothing and types of machine, to defensive and advanced riding techniques, there is something here for everyone.

Even though there are many dangers associated with riding motorcycles, our experience has taught us that if you are prepared to listen, learn and above all practise what you have been taught, motorcycling can continue to be not only a fun, but also a safe form of transport.

Safe riding!

PART ONE

BASIC TRAINING

BASIC TRAINING

This chapter introduces motorcycling in the form of the Compulsory Basic Training (CBT) syllabus. The first part of this chapter looks at what the law says, including the different types of licence available, the aims of CBT and advice on choosing the right equipment and clothing. The main features of different learner machines will be explained, including machine familiarization, basic checks and handling the machine. The second part of this chapter emphasizes the importance of basic machine skills and includes exercises that will help develop these skills as experienced during a CBT course. The last part of this chapter prepares the rider for the 'on-road' experience, including defensive riding, the effects of varying weather conditions and road surfaces and many other topics related to the motorcyclist and the road.

GETTING STARTED

SO YOU WANT TO RIDE A MOPED OR MOTORCYCLE

HERE'S WHAT THE LAW SAYS

All learner riders must hold a valid CBT Certificate

What the law says

The first step is to establish what type of licence you require, and what that licence allows you to ride.

Age 16 or over (first provisional)

You should apply for a provisional licence with moped entitlement. Upon completion of CBT, you will be entitled to ride a moped (see definition on page 7) with 'L' plates on your own. You will not be allowed to carry a pillion passenger or ride on motorways.

If you intend to ride a learner motorcycle on reaching the age of 17, make sure you request this when applying for your first provisional licence.

Age 17 or over

If this is your first provisional licence:

- you are entitled to apply for learner motorcycle entitlement;
- upon completing CBT you will be able to ride a learner motorcycle (see definition on page 8) with 'L' plates on your own while your licence and CBT are valid;
- you will not be allowed to carry a pillion passenger and ride on motorways;

- if you have not passed the motorcycle test within the two-year period, your motorcycle entitlement will expire. You will be able to get your learner motorcycle entitlement back on your licence after one year.

If you have obtained a full car licence you will be able to ride a moped without 'L' plates and be allowed to carry a pillion passenger. Upon completing CBT you will be entitled to ride a learner motorcycle (see definition on page 8) for as long as you have a valid CBT certificate.

Age 21 or over

Whether you hold a provisional or full car licence with learner motorcycle entitlement, you are entitled to ride a larger machine during CBT/Direct Access Scheme (DAS) when accompanied by an approved instructor; and wearing a fluorescent/reflective bib and instructed via an intercom on the road.

You are not allowed to ride machines over 125 cc on your own.

Definitions of mopeds and learner motorcycles

To be able to ride unaccompanied:

Moped

- is 50 cc or under;
- does not weigh more than 250 kg;
- has a maximum speed of approximately 30 mph (50 km per hour);
- is moved by pedals if manufactured before 1 August 1977.

Learner motorcycle

- is normally above 50 cc and less than 125 cc;
- is 14.6 bhp or below; and
- has a power output of 11 kw or less.

The aims of Compulsory Basic Training (CBT)

CBT was introduced in December 1990 to ensure that all first-time riders achieved a safe and competent level of riding before venturing onto the road on their own. CBT was also intended to reduce the number of accidents involving young and inexperienced motorcyclists. You must also complete CBT if you intend to apply for the Accompanied Motorcycle Test.

From 31 December 1996 all learner riders must take CBT before riding on the road. Full licence holders riding mopeds are exempt from taking CBT.

CBT format

To gain a CBT certificate you must reach a satisfactory standard in each of the five elements, A to E, which must be completed in sequence on the day. These elements will be summarized throughout this chapter. The exercises in each element do not have to be completed in sequence. You will only be able to proceed to the next element when your instructor is satisfied and when you are ready to do so. There are no time limits set during the course, although most training schemes will be able to give you a rough guide on how long it will last depending on your experience.

CBT is not a test. You will be assessed during the course. If you feel you are not ready to proceed onto the road you must make your feelings known.

Training ratios

CBT elements A to D will be completed off-road, in a group no larger than four trainees to one instructor (or two to one if taking the Direct Access route – see Chapter 2). For the final on-road element E, you should be in a group no larger than two trainees to one instructor. Ask to see your instructor's CBT licence. All qualified CBT instructors should carry their licence with them at all times during training.

Equipment and clothing

Motorcycle equipment and clothing have been designed for a purpose. It is very important that you buy the best that you can afford. You may find that the training scheme will be able to provide a helmet, gloves and possibly waterproofs for the day, although it is advisable to invest in a new helmet if you intend to continue your training. It is important that you dress sensibly for your CBT. Make sure you:

- are covered up, even if it is hot;
- take a protective jacket;
- wear good quality jeans if you do not have any motorcycle trousers;
- wear a pair of boots that at least cover your ankles.

Helmets

There are different styles and types of helmet to choose from. Whichever you decide to purchase, it must be an approved safety helmet displaying the BSI Kitemark, both on the helmet and the visor. It should also comply

with the British Standard BS6658 (1985) regulations.
(You will find 1985 stamped in all helmets. This is not
when the helmet was made, but when the British
Standard helmet regulations were introduced.)

The only people who are legally exempt from wearing a
helmet are those who wear a turban, usually members
of the Sikh religion.

Styles of helmets

There are basically two different styles of helmet, full-
face and open-face, although there is a helmet
available that includes a hinged chin section that can be
lifted to reveal your full face.

Full-face helmets

The advantages of having a full-face helmet are that it
fully protects your head, including the face and chin,
and offers protection from the weather.

Open-face helmets

Some people prefer open-face helmets supplemented
with goggles, which must also display the BSI
Kitemark.

Types of helmet

Helmets are classified as either Type A or Type B.

All helmets go through a series of safety tests to meet
the British Standard (BS) seal of approval. BS Type A
helmets (blue sticker) will have gone through a more
extensive testing procedure to that of the Type B (green
sticker). This does not mean that Type B helmets are any
less safe than Type A. Type A helmets will probably have
additional features that require more safety tests.

Helmet materials

Type A helmets usually represent the top end of the market, and are made with materials such as fibreglass, kevlar and carbon fibre that are very tough and tend to last longer when exposed to the elements. If not dropped or damaged, a Type A helmet should last for approximately five to seven years. The manufacturer will advise when to replace the helmet. The date of manufacture should be located on the helmet, somewhere! You will be able to affix stickers to this type of helmet as the glue on the sticker should not react with the helmet compound.

Type B helmets can be made with similar materials, but will more than likely be made from polycarbonate, take less time to make and will have a shorter life-span (approximately two to three years). If dropped or damaged, Type B helmets should be replaced immediately. They are not designed to have stickers stuck on them, as most solvents will weaken the polycarbonate compound.

If you have any doubts about the type, quality or length of life of a helmet, seek expert advice.

Visors and goggles

As well as displaying the BSI Kitemark, both visors and goggles must comply with one of the BS numbers listed below, which represent the extent of protection the visor or goggles will offer against small flying objects:

- BS4110 XA – low protection;
- BS4110 YA – medium protection;
- BS4110 ZA – good protection.

Scratched visors or goggles will distort your vision, particularly at night and in the rain. It is worth investing in anti-scratch visors or goggles as they will last longer.

Visors and goggles will probably mist or fog up in damp and wet weather. Your helmet should have a ventilation system, so make sure you know where the vents are and how to open them. There are also many anti-fog products available on the market that are worth considering. Visors can also be tinted to reduce glare. When purchasing a tinted visor, make sure it displays the BSI Kitemark.

Choosing a helmet

Whether you buy a Type A or B, make sure that you seek professional advice on helmet fitting. If a helmet is too loose it could come off; if it is too tight it will be uncomfortable and you may not be able to concentrate. Remember that the material inside the helmet will give after time. Make sure you make allowances for this. Different helmet materials will wear out at different rates.

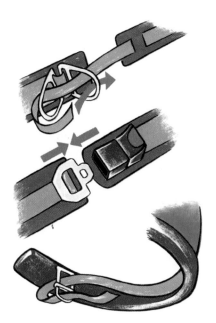

Safety straps

It is very important that you remember to fasten your safety strap properly. If the strap is not fastened properly the helmet could come off and you will be unsafe and breaking the law. There are three different types of safety strap:

- double D ring;
- quick release;
- bar and buckle.

Most helmets will also include Velcro or a snap button on the end of the strap to prevent the strap from flapping about in the wind. You must not use either to secure the helmet.

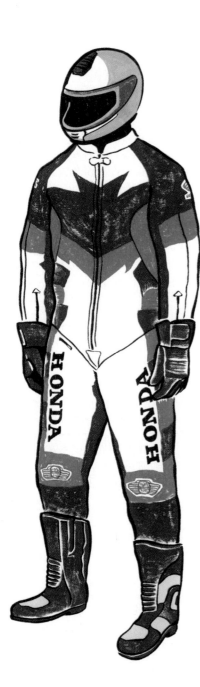

Clothing

Motorcycle clothing is specifically designed to:

- protect you from abrasion;
- ensure comfort and warmth;
- keep you dry.

There are different types and styles of clothing available on the market. It is important that you seek professional advice from the specialists. There are basically two types of clothing materials: 1) leather; and 2) man-made.

Leather

There are different levels of protection available. It is important when buying leather clothing that you look for a Genuine Leather or Cowhide label sewn into the garment.

Man-made

There are many different man-made materials available. Some offer protection as well as being waterproof. If the manufacturer claims that the garment will protect you from abrasion it should include a CE Mark. If any of these safety labels are missing it is worth considering separate body armour.

Eyesight requirements

If you have poor eyesight it is worth getting your eyesight checked before booking a CBT course. Your instructor will ask you to read a number plate at the start of your CBT. If you need glasses or contact lenses you must wear them on the day. If you cannot read the number plate correctly you will not be able to continue with the course. The number plate must contain letters and numbers of at least 79.4 millimetres (3.1 inches) high, and be at a distance of 20.5 metres (67 feet approximately).

Summary of introduction

- Aims of CBT.
- Importance of having the right equipment and clothing.
- Eyesight check.

Types of machine used

Whatever machine you decide to ride/purchase/hire, make sure you understand what type it is, and that it is legal and roadworthy.

Remember, if you are using your own machine for CBT, you are not legally allowed to ride your machine to the CBT site. You will not be covered by insurance even if you have a Certificate of Insurance. Insurance Certificates will only be valid during and upon completion of CBT. You must check that you will be insured during your CBT training.

There are many different styles of machine available, but there are basically two types of engine: two-stroke and four-stroke.

Two-stroke machines are usually associated with the smaller engines of 125 cc and below. They are generally simple in design and relatively easy to maintain. They will burn two-stroke oil as well as petrol, and they need regular maintenance.

A large proportion of machines available today are based on the four-stroke engine. It is also possible to obtain four-strokes in smaller engine sizes.

Types of machine

Mopeds/Scooters

These:

- are 50 cc or under;
- do not weigh more than 250 kg;
- have a maximum speed of 30 mph;
- are usually automatics, but geared mopeds are also available;
- are moved by pedals if registered before 1 August 1977;
- may be ridden without 'L' plates if the rider has a full moped licence.

Super-Scooters are available up to 250 cc.

Learner motorcycles

A common learner motorcycle:

- is above 50 cc and usually below 125 cc;
- has engine power output 14.6 bhp (11 kw) or below.

It is legal for learners to ride with 'L' plates.

Sports

These:

- are designed using racing technology, including race riding position;
- accelerate very quickly;
- are more expensive to buy, insure and run.

Touring

These:

- have armchair-style riding positions, and offer more weather protection;
- are designed for long-distance touring;
- have large engines and fuel tank capacity, and usually include luggage attachments.

Cruisers

These:

- have very comfortable riding positions;
- usually have very low seat heights;
- are designed for long, relaxing rides.

Trail bikes

These:

- are designed for the 'off-road' experience;
- need special suspension for ground clearance, and have increased seat height;
- have special tyres to improve traction when riding on rough ground;
- are larger machines equipped for longer distances.

Retro

These:

- bike without fairing;
- used for everyday riding;
- are easy to ride;
- have low running costs.

Familiarization with the machine's controls

Moped

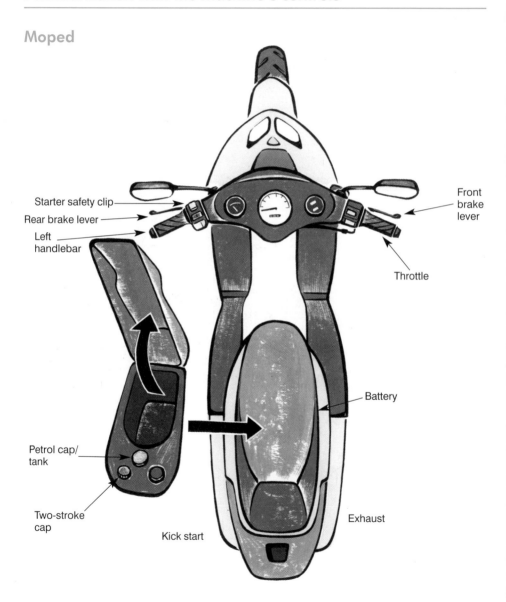

Starter safety clip

Rear brake lever

Left handlebar

Front brake lever

Throttle

Battery

Petrol cap/ tank

Two-stroke cap

Kick start

Exhaust

The figure on page 22 shows the location of controls, including:

(Moped)

Left side
- left handlebar
- rear brake lever
- kick-start
- starter safety clip on left side of machine

Right side
- front brake lever
- throttle
- exhaust

Centre
- petrol cap/tank
- two-stroke cap/reservoir
- battery

The figure on page 24 shows the location of controls, including:

(Geared)

Left side
- clutch lever
- petrol tap
- choke lever
- left footrest/gear selector

Right side
- front brake lever
- throttle
- kick-start
- exhaust
- right footrest/rear brake pedal

Centre
- petrol cap/tank

Geared

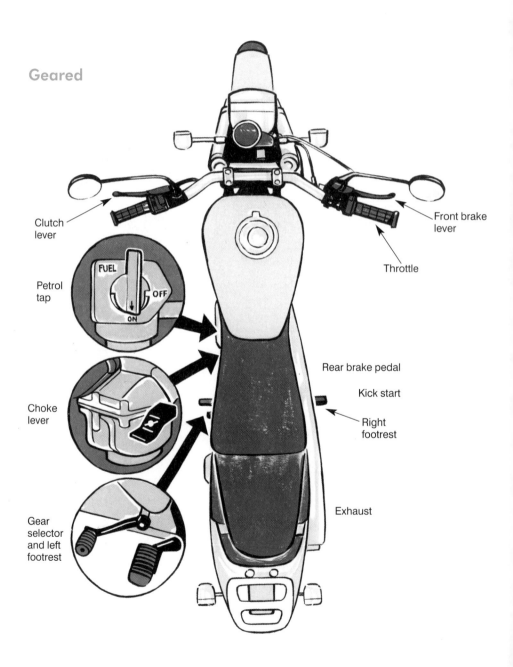

Clutch
lever

Petrol
tap

FUEL

OFF

ON

Choke
lever

Gear
selector
and left
footrest

Front brake
lever

Throttle

Rear brake pedal

Kick start

Right
footrest

Exhaust

Handlebars/clocks

(Geared)

Left side

- speedometer
- left turn indicator light
- clutch lever
- handlebar switches (lights, HI/LO beam, indicators, pass switch, horn)

Right side

- neutral (right turn) high beam indicator light
- temperature gauge
- front brake lever
- engine stop switch
- start switch
- throttle

Basic machine checks

It is important to check your machine for roadworthiness on a regular, daily basis and in more detail once a week. If there is a problem with your machine you are then more likely to notice it. Checking your machine on a regular basis will also help you plan your maintenance schedule.

Daily checks

Basic daily checks should only take about five minutes to complete. To make them easier to remember, the word *power* may be used.

Petrol Make sure you have sufficient fuel to complete your journey, or to reach your next fill-up point. Usually a visual check inside the petrol tank is required.

Oil If using a two-stroke machine, check two-stroke oil level. Two-stroke machines burn oil as well as petrol. If you run out of two-stroke oil, the engine will probably seize. Check four-stroke oil, gearbox oil levels.

Water/wheels If you are using a *water* cooled machine (the radiator is located at front of machine), check level. The coolant reservoir is usually located under the seat. Check condition of *wheels*, test *brakes* and check *chain* tension. This should be approximately half an inch to one inch play (see manual for accurate tension). Remember to spin the wheel and check all of the chain. It is possible that the chain may have developed a 'tight-spot'. Tight-spots indicate a seizure in the chain link, which could cause the chain to snap. Seek professional advice on replacement.

Electrics Turn key to the ON position to check instrument lights, headlight, rear light (some machines need to be running before the headlight/rear light will work), brake light, indicators and horn.

Rubber/tyres   Check for wear, cracks in side walls, pressure. Too much or too little will affect steering, handling and braking. Check depth of tread. The minimum tread depth requirement for mopeds should be visible, and 1 mm for motorcycles. Check with manufacturer for recommended tread depth. Look for nails and stones.

Weekly checks

Basic checks involve the safety of the machine for day-to-day running. Weekly checks are more detailed – you will be checking to see whether your machine requires any mechanical adjustments:

- check fuel system (is the fuel pipe properly fitted?) and the general condition of pipes/hoses;
- oil leaks/top-up levels;
- check condition of cables/levers and lubricate;
- check condition of wheels/spokes and make sure they are well balanced, not buckled;
- brakes – if drum- or cable-operated brakes, check wear indicator and adjust;
- brakes – if disc- or hydraulically-operated, check brake fluid level, brake pad wear;
- chain tension and adjustment/lubrication;
- battery fluid level check and top-up/charge if required;
- if shaft drive, check lubrication level;
- steering – check forks/head-stock bearings for play, trapped cables;
- loose nuts and bolts.

Always refer to owner's manual for correct adjustments.

On and off the stand

There are two basic types of stand; a centre stand and a side stand. Some machines include both. The centre stand is more stable and is very useful when carrying out basic machine checks and adjustments.

Putting the machine onto the centre stand:

- keep machine still with the front brake on and dismount machine to the left;
- both hands should remain on handle-bars, front brake still on, handle-bars straight;
- look down between arms to locate centre stand lever;
- lift right foot and push centre stand lever down onto ground;
- when two points of the centre stand are level on the ground, let go of front brake;

- keep two points on the ground, turn and face seat;
- with the right foot holding the machine still, encourage your right knee into the side panel for stability;
- find a suitable place to be able to lift the back end of the machine with your right hand (avoid using side panels, use grab handles if provided or part of the frame);
- co-ordinate your right foot and right hand, push down *hard* with your right foot, while lifting upwards and backwards with the right hand.

Avoid:

- trying to pull the machine onto the stand purely by pulling on the left handle-bar. Concentrate on using the centre stand lever, and push down with your right foot, lifting with your right hand at the same time;
- losing your balance. If the legs or two points of the centre stand are not level on the ground the machine will be unstable. Avoid putting the machine on to the centre stand on uneven surfaces;
- putting the machine onto the centre stand on a hill, slight cambers and recently laid tarmac in hot weather, as you may find it very difficult to take off afterwards;
- sitting on the machine while on the stand. The stand is only designed to take the weight of the machine.

Taking the machine off the centre stand

- Make sure the handle-bars are straight, and hold onto the left handle-bar grip with your left hand.
- Cover the centre stand lever with your right foot (left foot is acceptable if preferred, although you will not be able to step forward once the machine is off the stand).

- With your right hand hold grab rail or handle if provided, or suitable fixed part of back end of machine.

- Lift back end of your machine upwards and forward so that it is able to tilt forward off the stand. If the machine is very heavy it may be easier to 'bounce' the machine off its stand. Using your right hand push down on rear grab handle and as it bounces back, pull forward. Be careful not to put too much effort into the bounce!

- As your machine starts to tilt forward and is beyond the pivot point, apply pressure on the centre stand lever with your right foot. This will ensure that the machine will reach the ground, gently and without rolling forward.

- Once the machine is on the ground, tilt it slightly towards you, apply the front brake and release the centre stand lever gently.

> ### Point to Remember
>
> If you experience difficulties getting the machine to pivot off the centre stand:
>
> - This is usually because of too much pressure on the centre stand lever. Remember to cover the centre stand lever to begin with. Only apply pressure once the machine starts to move forward.
> - Some light machines, usually mopeds, will not pivot off the centre stand even if there is the slightest pressure on the centre stand lever. In this case it is acceptable to put your right foot in front of the centre stand. This will also prevent the machine from dragging forward when pulling from the rear.
> - If you nearly lose your balance once the machine reaches the ground, you may have let go of the centre stand too early and before the front brake lever is applied. It could be that the machine is on a slight slope, which will cause the machine to naturally fall. Make sure you keep your foot on the lever, even after the machine has reached the ground. The stand will act as a brake and keep the machine stable.

Putting the machine onto the side stand

- Dismount your machine to the left, keep hands on handle-bars, front brake on.
- Locate side stand and open out as far as it will go.
- Rest the machine gently onto the stand and turn handle-bars to the left.

Avoid putting the machine onto the side stand on uneven ground or recently laid tarmac in hot weather. Make sure the ground is solid when using the side stand.

Taking the machine off the side stand

Stand on the left side of the machine, hands on handlebars and apply the front brake. Straighten machine and retract side stand.

Avoid sitting astride the machine, with the side stand down. This could be very dangerous, especially if the machine does not have a cut-out switch, which kills the engine if you try to pull away with the side stand down. It is safer to get into the habit of always retracting the stand before getting on your machine.

Handling the machine

When pushing your machine in a straight line or manoeuvring the machine to the left and right, it is important to maintain balance and stability. Even the lightest machine can appear heavy when falling!

Wheeling the machine to the left and right

Standing on the left-hand side of the machine, tilt the machine slightly towards you, resting the tank or the side of the seat on the right side of your body. Turning left and right keep the machine in this position. Take slow, short steps.

Avoid turning too quickly and not keeping the machine close to you, as this could make you and your machine unstable. Also, avoid applying the front brake while turning, as this is very dangerous and will almost certainly cause you to lose your balance. Try to straighten the machine before you bring it to a controlled halt, and apply the brake gently.

Starting and stopping the engine

There is a safe and systematic way of starting the engine, and it is safer to be sitting astride the machine. To make this process easier to remember, the word *pigs* may be used.

Petrol   Make sure that the petrol tap has been turned to the ON position. If the machine is cold it may require choke.

Ignition   Turn the key to the ON position. (Remember that turning the key will not start the engine.)

Gear   Check that the machine is in neutral. If the neutral light is not on but you think you are in neutral then push the machine forward. If it rolls forward freely

you are in neutral (remember not to pull the clutch in!). If the machine will not move forward you will be in gear. It is dangerous to try to start the machine when in gear.

Starting the engine

Kick start

If your machine has a kick start, you will need to move the kick-start lever into position. With your right foot on the lever proceed to start the engine with a quick downward movement.

Let the kick-start lever return, and repeat this movement until the engine starts. Once started, return the lever to its resting position. Some machines may need some throttle at the beginning. When the engine is warm, turn the choke to the OFF position if used.

Electric start

If your machine has an electric start, simply press the button. When the engine is warm it should tick-over without choke.

Automatic machine

Most automatic machines will only start if one or both of the brakes are applied.

Stopping the engine

- throttle off;
- make sure the machine is in neutral;
- turn the key in the ignition to the OFF position;
- switch the fuel tap to the OFF position if leaving the machine for any length of time (some machines have vacuum-operated carburettors that enable the fuel tap to be left on continually).

Some machines have an engine stop switch. This switch must only be used in an emergency.

Summary of practical on-site riding

- Familiarization of motorcycle and its controls.
- Ability to carry out basic machine checks.
- Taking the machine on and off the stand.
- Wheeling the machine to the left and to the right.
- Bringing the machine to a controlled halt by braking.
- Ability to start and stop the engine.

MOVING ON

Moving off and stopping (geared machine)

Make sure that the engine is warm and ticking over with the throttle and choke closed:

- with front brake applied, pull the clutch lever *in*;
- select first gear (usually one click down); make sure the clutch lever is kept *in* during gear selection; cover the rear brake lever with your right foot;

- release the front brake lever;
- release the clutch lever *slowly* until the engine speed begins to drop and the machine starts to move slowly forward. Increase the throttle slightly and hold;
- you have now reached the 'biting point' of the clutch;
- pull the clutch lever *in* and throttle off.

Repeat this exercise several times to familiarize yourself with the feel of the biting point:

- to be able to move forward, find the biting point and increase the throttle slightly and allow the machine to move forward;
- once moving keep the clutch on the biting point and release *slowly* while increasing the throttle gently;
- after moving a few metres, and once you have your balance, lift your feet and gently find the footrests;
- throttle off – apply brakes gently – and pull clutch in (during very slow speeds you may find you have to pull the clutch in before applying the brakes, to avoid stalling the engine);
- repeat this exercise and remember to look ahead. Practise riding the machine by listening and feeling.

Avoid letting the clutch out quickly as this may cause you to 'bolt' forward, lose control and possibly stall the engine.

Moving off and stopping (automatic machine)

- release brakes;
- turn throttle very slowly until you feel a sudden surge forward;
- do not be alarmed at the sudden surge and increase the throttle;
- it is easier to pull away and increase the throttle straight away as it will help you get your balance;
- once you have your balance lift your feet and gently rest them on the footrests or in front of you on the machine;
- after travelling a few metres, throttle off and apply brakes gently;
- remember to keep the brakes on while stationary and while the engine is running.

Repeat this exercise several times.

Slow riding (geared machine)

This exercise will help you control your machine while riding among slow-moving traffic on the road:

- pull away as you would normally;
- once you are well balanced, throttle off and slow the machine down;
- when you feel that you are about to lose your balance, retrieve the clutch and find the biting point again and increase the throttle slightly;
- *ride* the clutch on the biting point (*riding* or *slipping the clutch* can be achieved by holding the clutch on the biting point and only allowing it to move a few millimetres at a time either way depending on whether you need to increase/decrease speed);
- if slow riding on a slight slope or turn, it is safer and easier to slow the machine down by *gentle use of the*

rear brake only. The rear brake may be used in these situations, however it is not good practice to rely on this brake on its own during normal riding conditions;

- riding the clutch can cause the machine to overheat. Practise slow riding for only a few minutes at a time.

Controlled braking

This exercise highlights the effectiveness of your brakes under controlled braking. It simulates braking as experienced when approaching junctions and traffic lights. This is a valuable exercise as it can take time and practice to understand and achieve good co-ordination of both brakes.

While travelling in a straight line, in an upright position, with a good, dry surface:

- apply front brake slightly before rear;
- apply more pressure to the front, approximately 75 per cent pressure to the front brake lever, 25 per cent to the rear;
- brake progressively, and if you have not locked any of the wheels, keep the brakes on until you have stopped. Then ease off the brakes once you have come to a halt to make it a smoother stop;
- if riding a geared machine remember to pull the clutch in before stopping to avoid stalling the engine.

If riding on a wet surface apply both brakes gently, using 25 per cent pressure to the front brake lever, 25 per cent to the rear.

When riding on poor road surfaces, for example, oil, diesel, ice, grit, gravel, wet leaves, etc, throttle-off and use engine braking, gears and, as a last resort *only*, apply the rear brake, gently.

When approaching a bend make sure you adjust your speed before you enter it. It is dangerous to brake during a bend, particularly with the front brake. If you have to slow down on a bend use engine braking, and *only* apply the rear brake, gently.

Avoid stamping hard on the rear brake as this will almost certainly cause the back wheel to lock and cause a skid. If you do lock the rear wheel, release the rear brake immediately and re-apply gently. Practise applying the rear brake gently with a movement from the ankle.

Causes of a skid

A skid can be caused by one or a combination of the following: excessive acceleration, harsh braking, or leaning too low for the prevailing conditions. If your machine starts to skid, remove the cause. Avoid making the skid worse by adding another cause.

Gear changing

The best way to understand gear changing is to think about riding a push bike. When you set off on a push bike you are usually in first gear. This gear gets you moving quite quickly. After travelling a few metres in this gear, particularly on level ground, you will find that you are pedalling very fast but not getting very far. Changing up into second gear enables you to build more speed, but your legs seem to be pedalling at half

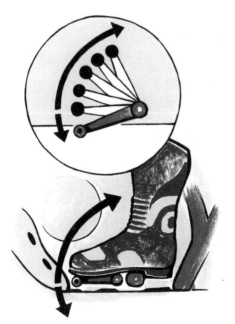

the speed, and it is harder to pedal. As you build your speed you will need to change up to the next gear and so on. When you start to slow down almost to a halt, if you have not changed down during this time you will find that you will not be able turn the pedals, as it will be too hard to get going again.

Gear selector

Motorcycles have sequential gears. You will not be able to change from fifth gear to first in one movement. Gear selection is made by shifting the gear lever either up or down, and then letting the lever return to its resting position, usually a horizontal position.

Building speed – changing up

Before attempting the gear change for the first time, make sure you have a good, long, straight stretch of smooth, quiet land to practise on. If you are practising on a slight slope, then it is easier to ride down the slope first:

- with engine running, select first gear and pull away;
- build speed and prepare your left foot ready for the gear change by placing it under the gear lever;
- prepare to co-ordinate clutch, throttle and gears;
- at the same time, pull the *clutch in*, take the *throttle off* and *change up* into second gear with the gear lever and then let the gear lever return to its resting place;
- gently let the clutch out and turn the throttle on, simultaneously.

Avoid:

- pulling the clutch in before taking the throttle off. This will make the engine rev high and will probably make you lose your concentration;
- taking the throttle off before pulling the clutch in. Your machine will slow down very quickly and by the time you have changed up into second gear you will probably be moving too slowly for that gear and the machine will struggle.

Point to Remember

Get your gear-changing foot in place before your hands are ready. This will help with your co-ordination of all three at the same time. Make the gear-changing process a smooth and quick one. The longer you take to change up, the harder it will be to get moving. Listen to the engine; if it is racing it is time to change up.

Slowing down – changing down

- *throttle off*, consider using your brakes, pull the *clutch in* and select lower gear by pressing the gear lever down and letting the lever return to its resting place;
- at the same time, let the *clutch out* slowly and turn *throttle on*;
- listen to the engine; if it is struggling, change down a gear.

Avoid changing down into a lower gear before slowing down. This may cause the vehicle to skid. Always match engine speed with the appropriate gear.

Figure of eight

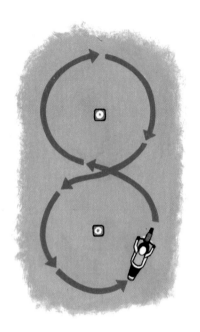

This exercise is designed to develop your clutch control and stability while turning at slow speeds. It will also encourage you to look around, as experienced when turning left and right out of junctions:

- place two cones apart, start at a slight angle ready to ride through the gap;
- pull away and establish your balance, and try to control your speed before starting the first circle by riding the clutch on the biting point;
- remember to keep glancing at your target, the centre of the cones;
- if riding on a slope certain parts of the figure of eight will probably be faster than others. If you feel you are going too fast, use your rear brake gently to slow the machine down, to give you more stability;
- if you sense that the machine is struggling and you feel you are about to lose your balance, you will need to increase the throttle slightly;
- you may also want to try moving your body weight in the opposite way you are circling, to help your balance.

Avoid

- small circles to begin with. Start big and work smaller. Only attempt three or four at a time, otherwise you may feel dizzy and lose your balance altogether;
- using your front brake during this exercise;

- looking down. You will not be able to complete the figure of eight if you are not glancing at your target and the cones.

Emergency stop

Hopefully, you will never have to do an emergency stop. However, it is worth practising so that you know what to do. During your CBT the instructor will signal you to do an emergency stop while you are travelling in an upright position, in a straight line:

- Try not to grab the front brake too hard, or stamp on the rear brake during this exercise. This exercise is designed to improve your reaction to the situation.
- Apply the front brake slightly before the rear. Apply 75 per cent pressure to the front, 25 per cent to the rear if the surface is dry and clear. Even out the pressures if the ground is wet.
- Only pull the clutch in just before you stop. The engine braking will help the machine come to a halt safely and quickly.
- Once you have stopped, remember that you may have to change down through the gear box a few times to get back to first.

Rear observations

A rear observation is made to see and register in your mind what is happening behind you. Using your mirrors will sometimes be adequate. At other times you will need to follow this through with a look over your shoulder to cover your blind area or to make other road users more aware of your actions. Some mirrors are convex to give you a wider view, but these will give you a false reading of speed and distances.

Sitting astride your machine, with your instructor or friend directly behind you at a distance:

- adjust your mirrors so that you can see this person clearly;
- ask the person to walk towards the back of your machine, slightly to the right;
- tell the person to stop walking when he or she disappears in your mirrors. This is the blind area.

There will be times when you will need to look over your shoulder to view your blind area, for example when changing course or direction.

Considering lifesavers

The last look you take before you manoeuvre is known as a lifesaver. If you intend to deviate or turn to the left, consider taking a lifesaver to the left before you turn, and if you intend to deviate or turn to the right, consider taking a lifesaver to the right before you turn.

Consider taking a lifesaver in the following situations:

- before committing yourself to a manoeuvre when you are not sure if there is anything in your blind spot;
- when there is a cycle lane clearly marked on the left-hand side of the road and you are turning left;
- if you anticipate a cyclist or another motorcyclist filtering to the front of a long queue, before you move away and before turning;
- before deviating or turning right, particularly in a busy, built-up area and when turning right into a minor side road.

Avoid

- looking too many times. If you have to look twice, one observation after another, you may not notice what is happening in front of you in time. It also reveals that you probably did not look properly the first time;
- rear observations during a bend. You will probably lose your balance and position;
- rear observations while following slow-moving traffic. The traffic in front may stop suddenly;
- rear observations at the time when you should be concentrating on the traffic flow.

Point to Remember

When you are aware of what is happening behind you, it is safer to concentrate on the road ahead, particularly when travelling at high speeds along quieter roads. Decide where and when a lifesaver is necessary. Use your mirrors regularly to keep up to date with what is behind you.

U-turn manoeuvre

This exercise requires all the skills that you will have developed during the slow riding and figure of eight. It simulates what you must consider when wanting to change direction on a road:

- when considering a U-turn manoeuvre make sure you can see up and down the road clearly;
- start close to the kerb on the left-hand side of the road;
- select first gear;
- look ahead, in your mirrors, and then over your right shoulder;

- signal right if you feel there is another road user who will benefit from it (that includes pedestrians);
- if the road is clear, pull forward and get your balance (if you have travelled along the road for some distance you should take a lifesaver check to see that it is safe to continue);
- if the road is still clear, ride the clutch on the biting point, keep engine revving at the same point and start to turn the steering to the right;
- once three-quarters of the way around, look up and around to the right. Focus on a stopping point to give you stability (it is easier to identify something to focus on before you begin this manoeuvre);
- once you have completed the turn, bring the machine to a gentle stop, or take a lifesaver check to see if it is safe to continue. Cancel your indicator if used;
- practise pulling off and turning straight away.

Avoid

- attempting to complete a U-turn on a bend, among parked high-sided vehicles – anywhere that restricts your vision;
- using the front brake during this manoeuvre. Applying the front brake will almost certainly cause you to lose your balance and put your foot down;
- looking at the kerb. If you look at the kerb you will probably be heading for it. If you think you are going to hit the kerb, you will probably panic and apply the brakes;
- straightening or playing with the steering during the turn. You will need to turn and hold the steering to be able to complete a safe manoeuvre.

Right and left turns (observation–signal–manoeuvre, position–speed–look routines)

During your CBT you will be shown a safe way of turning left and right. It is important to understand each individual action and that the whole procedure is to be used as a guide. It may not always be practical to complete the whole procedure.

Turning right

- Start with a mirror check, and proceed with a rear observation over the right shoulder (if there is a vehicle behind you, you may consider delaying your signal).
- Signal right.
- Consider taking another rear observation, a lifesaver check to the right (if there is another vehicle closing on you, wait until that vehicle has passed and take another check).
- If it is clear behind you, manoeuvre to just left of the centre line (use the edge of your mirrors as a guide).
- Check mirrors, adjust speed and gears and consider taking a lifesaver check over the right shoulder before looking right and left at the end of the road.
- Once you have made the decision that it is safe to proceed with the manoeuvre, focus on looking into the road that you are moving into (see Road Junctions, page 89).
- If it is unsafe to proceed, turn your head to the front and continue braking to a safe stop just before the 'give way' lines. If you are still looking to the side when you come to a halt, you will probably lose your balance.

- Once it is safe to go, consider taking another life-saver check before you move off.

Turning left

- Mirror check, and proceed with a rear observation over your right shoulder.
- Signal left.
- Mirror check, and if there is a vehicle closing on you, you may consider another rear observation.
- Adjust speed, gears and consider a lifesaver check over your left shoulder to make sure that it will be safe to manoeuvre into position for the left turn. Make sure that there are no pedal cyclists travelling on the inside.
- Once you have made the decision that it is safe to proceed, look left into the road, before moving into it (see Road Junctions, page 89).
- If you had to give way to another vehicle and stop, remember to consider another lifesaver as a safe gap emerges. Focus on the road you are moving into before pulling away.

Avoid

- looking too many times. If you have to look twice, one observation after another, you may not notice what is happening in front of you in time. It also reveals that you probably did not look properly the first time;

- rear observations during a bend. You will probably lose your balance and position;
- rear observations while following slow-moving traffic. The traffic in front may stop suddenly;
- rear observations at the time when you should be concentrating on the traffic flow at junctions and roundabouts;
- trying to complete the above procedures when you clearly have not got the time or distance to fit everything in. Remember the basics – observation–signal–manoeuvre.

Summary of practical on-site riding

- Ride the machine under control in a straight line.
- Bring the machine to a controlled halt.
- Ride the machine round a figure of eight.
- Be able to ride the machine slowly under control.
- Carry out controlled braking using both brakes correctly.
- Be able to stop as in an emergency.
- Change gear safely and correctly.
- Carry out a U-turn.
- Carry out rear observations.
- Be able to turn left and right correctly using the observation–signal–manoeuvre routine and the position–speed–look routine.

RIDING ON THE ROAD

Understanding the Highway Code

To be able to ride on the road you need to obey the rules. The Highway Code is the road user's manual, and is designed to prevent accidents. It is important to understand what is included in the Highway Code, so that we all adopt the same rules on the road.

Defensive riding

Defensive riding includes most of what is mentioned in this section. A defensive rider will observe and plan well ahead, and anticipate the actions of other road users.

- Although the driver on the roundabout is signalling left to exit the roundabout, the rider has anticipated that the driver might have made a mistake and indicated too early, and is actually carrying on round the roundabout.
- The rider noticed that the car wheels were slightly turned to the right, which is inconsistent with what the driver was actually intending to do.

Effective use of rear observations

A rear observation over your shoulder covers the area that you cannot see in your mirrors. A look over your shoulder will also warn other road users that you may be about to change course. You should only consider a rear observation over your shoulder when you know what is happening in front of you.

- The rider observes a parked car ahead.
- After taking a look in the mirrors, the rider decides to take a rear observation over the shoulder.
- The vehicle following delays overtaking the motorcyclist.

Correct road position

The correct road position is a safe position and will vary depending on:

- what type of road you are travelling along;
- the road width;
- the condition of the surface;
- if there are any vehicles in front or behind;
- if there are any obstructions ahead.

Safe position on the road

Where possible, the safest position on the road is the centre of your lane (unless there is an accumulation of oil or diesel on the ground). This position clears you from any drains or rubbish in the gutter, and provides a safe distance away from any oncoming vehicles.

Following other vehicles

You must always be able to stop safely in the distance you can see to be clear. The Highway Code includes the shortest stopping distances in feet, metres and in car lengths. As a rough guide, the 'two-second rule' can be applied.

- When following another vehicle, find a fixed object ahead of the vehicle in front.
- When the vehicle in front passes the fixed object say to yourself slowly 'only a fool breaks the two-second rule', or count '1,001, 1,002'. If you pass the fixed object and you are still saying the phrase or still counting, then you are too close.
- You must at least double your braking distance in wet conditions.

Riding in traffic

When riding in traffic, particularly when the traffic is moving slowly, it is important to remember your safety distance. There is often a temptation to move off at the same time as the vehicle in front. When in a queue of traffic:

- always leave at least a bike's length between you and the vehicle in front when stationary. This will give you enough space if the vehicle in front starts to reverse or if you need to manoeuvre around the vehicle;
- give yourself a delay when pulling away. The larger the vehicle, the longer the delay;

- always make sure you can see ahead, and be seen by the driver in front.

Avoid pulling away at the same time as the vehicle in front. If the vehicle in front pulls away slowly, you will be forced to stop very quickly, and you will be too close once you have stopped.

Point to Remember

When pulling away on a motorcycle you will need a certain speed to be able to maintain your balance.

Filtering

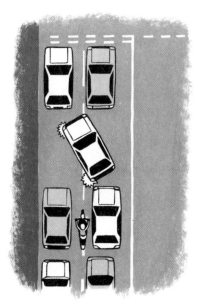

It is not uncommon to see motorcyclists filtering between lines of traffic. It is very dangerous to weave among traffic, particularly when the traffic is moving.

When in a traffic queue, it is possible that the drivers are not anticipating a motorcyclist filtering amongst them, and they may decide to:

- change lane suddenly;
- let another vehicle into the queue from a side road;
- leave enough space for a pedestrian or cyclist to cross in front of them.

This type of filtering is not recommended.

Varying weather conditions

All weather conditions will affect your riding in some way. It is important to understand how these conditions will affect you, your concentration and machine handling. Weather conditions to be considered in more detail are:

- hot weather;
- rain;
- wind;
- fog and mist;
- snow and ice.

Hot weather

If you are 'hot and bothered' you will probably lose your concentration. Make sure that your clothing keeps you cool and avoid wearing man-made materials that do not breathe. Although it is easier and more enjoyable to ride during hot weather, you will still need to be wearing protective clothing.

Riding during bright sunshine will cause you to squint, which after a period of time will make you feel very tired. Direct sunlight will also:

- make it difficult to see the road ahead;
- make it difficult for other road users to see you;
- reflect objects if the surface is wet, making it very difficult to judge hazards.

Long periods of very intense heat may cause the road surface to melt. Melted tar can stick to your tyres and in severe cases can cause you to skid. Melted tar can be particularly dangerous while accelerating, braking and cornering. When it rains after a long spell of hot weather, the road surface will be slippery and will require extreme caution.

Rain

If you are not wearing waterproof clothing during wet conditions you will feel cold and uncomfortable after a short period of time. You may find it difficult to concentrate and operate the controls. Riding in the rain also makes it difficult to see and be seen, and increases the chances of skidding.

Riding in the rain

Make sure you are familiar with the ventilation system on your helmet. Opening the vents will increase the air flow in the helmet, and will prevent the visor from misting up. Alternatively you can purchase anti-fog sprays or a shield. When riding in the rain:

- avoid excessive acceleration, braking and leaning;
- brake gently, and apply less pressure on the front. Even out the braking pressures to 25 per cent front and 25 per cent rear;
- braking will be less efficient. It will take longer to stop and you will need to at least double your braking distance;
- avoid riding over manhole covers on a bend and whilst leaning, braking or accelerating.

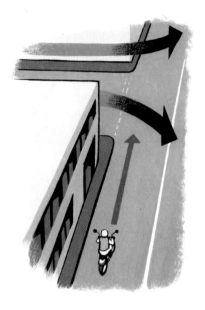

Wind

You should always ride at a speed at which you are able to control the machine. Strong crosswinds can blow you and other road users off course. Crosswinds can be anticipated when:

- travelling along exposed roads;
- passing high-sided vehicles;
- in between buildings and when approaching side roads.

Fog and mist

If you have to travel in fog or mist, allow more time for your journey. Riding in fog and mist will:

- make you feel cold and damp. Wear waterproof clothing to keep you dry and warm;
- make it difficult to see and be seen. Ride with your dipped beam, and adjust your speed so that you will be able to stop safely within the distance you can see. Pay more attention to signs and road markings, as they will help you negotiate the next section of road;
- cause the inside and outside of your visor or goggles to mist up. You will need to wipe your visor clear on a regular basis;
- make the approach to junctions more dangerous. Adjust your speed in the anticipation of a vehicle emerging.

Avoid following tail lights. There is no guarantee that the person in front is able to see any better than you, and he or she may brake suddenly.

Snow and ice

Only ride in these conditions if you really have to. If snow is forecast you may find that the main roads have been gritted the night before. If riding on snow:

- travel very slowly and avoid any sudden movements;
- try to slow down in plenty of time using engine braking, gears and only the rear brake to bring you to a halt;
- if safe to do so, take a wider turn at junctions, as the kerbs will be concealed from you;
- try to anticipate what could be underneath the snow;
- signs and road markings will probably be covered. Remember that the 'give way' and 'stop' signs are unique, and although covered in snow their shape will help you decide what to do.

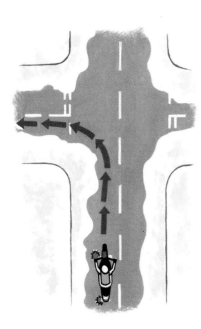

In freezing conditions:

- avoid travelling close to places that use water frequently. If riding on black ice you will not hear the tyre noise, and you will not have any tyre grip;
- try to avoid any sudden movements and let the machine slow down gradually. It is dangerous to brake on ice;
- your hands and feet will feel the cold very quickly. Wear plenty of thin layers of clothing to help keep the heat in. Plan lots of stops to warm up.

Road surfaces

You will need to be aware of the different types of road surface that can be encountered, and how they will affect your riding. You must be on the look-out for:

- tar banding;
- potholes;
- inspection covers;
- oil and diesel spillages;
- painted white lines and markings;
- cattle grids, railway and tram lines;
- loose chippings, gravel, mud and leaves.

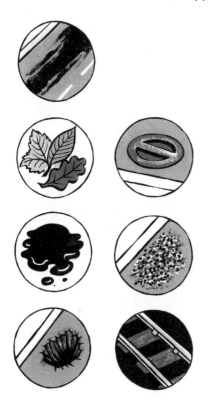

If you have to ride over any of the surfaces mentioned above, avoid accelerating, braking and leaning. Slippery surfaces are more likely to cause you to lose control and skid. It is possible to anticipate a slippery surface and be able to avoid it, or be able to slow down in time before riding over it. Be observant:

- the rider is approaching a built-up area, and notices trees lining the road through the village;
- the rider is anticipating that the surface may still be wet as the sun has not been able to penetrate through the trees;
- the rider is also expecting a surface covered in leaves.

Use of conspicuity aids

Motorcycles are more difficult to see than most other vehicles on the road. It is important to be seen and to do everything you can to help other road users see you. You should consider:

- riding with your headlight on dipped beam;
- wearing fluorescent clothing/accessories during the day;
- wearing reflective clothing/accessories during night riding.

Legal requirements

The legal requirements for riding on the road will apply to you as a rider. You will also be responsible for the legal requirements for your machine.

You must:

- be fit and able to ride, and your eyesight must be to the required standard;
- hold a valid driving licence, with the appropriate entitlement;
- hold a CBT certificate (if required);
- wear an approved safety helmet.

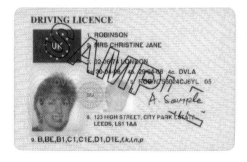

Your machine must:

- have a valid insurance certificate;
- have Vehicle Excise Duty (a valid tax disc, if applicable);
- have an MOT certificate (if applicable);
- have 'L' plates front and rear (if required).
- be in good condition and of working order at all times (roadworthiness).

Vulnerability

Motorcyclists have less physical protection than drivers inside a vehicle, and are less visible (approximately only a third of the width of an average-sized car). Motorcycles are also less stable, and are more likely to skid than any other vehicle.

Ride according to the road and traffic conditions

Only ride up to the speed limit if it is safe to do so. It is important to travel at a speed that enables you to comfortably take in all the information around you. At higher speeds you will have less time to react. Consider the following:

- The rider approaches a built-up area, and can see in the distance the main shopping area, where there is a lot of activity.
- Although there is a 30 mph restriction in force, the rider decides to slow down and prioritize the hazards.
- All hazards can be potentially dangerous, although it is good practice to identify which ones are more serious.
- Always travel at a speed that enables you to cope with the information needed to progress safely.

Consequences of aggressive attitudes

With the increase in the volume of traffic over the last few years, it is not uncommon to witness or experience some form of road-rage. If you respond to a road-rage situation, you may be putting yourself, and other road users, in danger. Try to avoid conflict with other road users, and remember to remain calm. It is important that you retain the level of concentration required to deal with the situation safely. In desperate situations you may decide that it will be safer to pull over and let the following vehicle pass.

Hazard perception

A hazard can be:

- physical or fixed features, including junctions, bends, cambers, parked cars and so on;
- other road users travelling along the road;
- changes in the environment, including weather and surface variations.

Approaching a bend

There are a number of factors that must be considered before entering a bend:

- is there an obstruction around the corner?
- possible changes in the surface condition, weather and environment;
- speed on approach.

After taking everything into consideration, you should always make sure that:

- any speed changes occur before the bend;
- after entering, keep a steady, consistent throttle speed;
- you are always able to stop safely within the distance you can see to be clear.

The ability to spot a hazard in plenty of time to be able to react to it is a skill and will improve with experience. If you are in the right place, at the right time, travelling at the correct speed for the conditions and have a safe distance between you and the vehicle in front, you should be able to spot and deal with hazards safely.

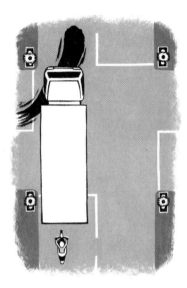

Consider the following:

- the rider is too close to the lorry, is unable to see the traffic lights changing and is unaware of the diesel spillage ahead;
- the driver is unaware that there is a motorcyclist following;
- the motorcyclist cannot see the driver in the lorry's mirrors;
- if the driver suddenly stopped, the motorcyclist would be unable to stop safely in time.

The effects of drugs and alcohol

Certain illegal drugs and alcohol will almost certainly affect your concentration and ability to react in time. Some legal prescription drugs can make you drowsy and unfit for riding. Always read the label and if in doubt seek advice from a chemist, or contact your doctor.

Drinking and riding is not sensible. Although the law states a maximum level of 80 milligrams of alcohol per 100 millilitres of blood, this level will still slow your reactions. It is not safe to drink and ride.

Summary of practical on-road training

Before going out onto the road your instructor will explain the need to:

- recognize the importance of reading *The Highway Code;*
- ride defensively and anticipate the action of other road users;
- use rear observations at appropriate times;
- assume the correct road position when riding;
- leave sufficient space when following another vehicle;
- pay due regard to varying weather conditions;
- be aware of the effect on a vehicle of the different types of road surface that can be encountered;
- be aware of the need to be clearly visible to other road users (see the use of conspicuity aids, page 64)
- recognize the legal requirements for riding on the road;
- understand why motorcyclists are more vulnerable than most road users;
- drive at the correct speed according to the road and traffic conditions;
- be aware of the consequences of aggressive attitudes when riding;
- be aware of the importance of hazard perception;
- be aware of the dangers of drug and alcohol use.

Summary of practical on-road riding

You will be taken out onto the road for a minimum period of two hours and should cover all of the following traffic situations:

- roundabouts;
- junctions;
- pedestrian crossings;
- traffic lights;
- gradients;
- bends;
- obstructions.

You will also be expected to repeat on-road the following exercises:

- the U-turn manoeuvre;
- the emergency stop.

The Certificate of Completion

681653

DRIVING STANDARDS AGENCY

Road Traffic Act 1988

Certificate of Completion of an Approved Training Course for Motor Vehicles in Categories A and P

Driver Number of Candidate

Hrs Mins

Date and Time of Course Completion

Current Name

Current Address

Postcode

has successfully completed an approved training course for motor vehicles in categories A and P, prescribed for the purpose of Section 97 of the Road Traffic Act 1988 as amended by Section 6 of the Road Traffic (Driver Licensing and Information Systems) Act 1989.

Appointed to conduct such training

Signature of Instructor

No.

Initials and surname (BLOCK CAPITALS)

The successful candidate should sign in ink below in the presence of the instructor.

Address of site at which Course conducted

Signature

Official Stamp of Training Body

Site No.

DL 196 Rev (1/94)

Please read the notes overleaf

An Executive Agency of the Department of Transport

When you have completed the CBT course to a satisfactory standard, you will be issued a Certificate of Completion of the Approved Training Course for Motor Vehicles in Categories A and P (DL196 CBT Certificate). This certificate:

- validates your provisional motorcycle/moped entitlement on your licence;

- entitles you to ride on the road on your own;

- is valid for a three-year period from the date and time of issue;

- is also the first part to passing the DSA practical motorcycle or moped test, after completing the theory test (if applicable).

PART TWO

TRAINING TO PASS YOUR TEST

TRAINING TO PASS YOUR TEST

The first part of this chapter looks at the stages in preparing for your test and offers advice on the different training courses that are available. This section also looks at hiring a machine, and includes useful tips when buying. The Direct Access Scheme is explained, including familiarization with the larger machine and exercises to improve basic manoeuvres. The second part of the chapter deals with riding on the road, and starts by explaining the different types of roads and road junctions. Many road systems and rules are covered, including dealing with box junctions and bus lanes. The chapter concludes by providing information about taking the test, including what to expect, documentation requirements, end of test questions and the end result.

LICENSING LAWS – THEORY TEST

If you are a provisional licence holder, and intend to apply for the moped/motorcycle practical test, you must apply for and pass the moped/motorcycle theory test first before booking a practical moped/motorcycle test. It is advisable to book your theory test plenty of time before your intention to train for your practical test, as you need to allow for a re-take if you do not reach the required standard. The Theory Test Pass Certificate is valid for three years. If you do not take your practical test within this time you must re-take the theory test. For more details contact the Driving Standards Agency (DSA).

Full licence holders are exempt from taking the Theory Test.

Licensing laws

Basically there are three types of full licence: 1) a full moped licence; 2) a light (Category A1) motorcycle licence; and 3) a standard (Category A) motorcycle licence.

Moped – Will allow you to discard your 'L' plates and carry a pillion passenger.

Light (A1) – If your aim is to ride a motorcycle and you decide to pass your test on a machine between 75 cc and 125 cc, on passing you will be restricted to machines of up to 125 cc (11 kw power output or 14.6 bhp).

Standard (A) – If your intentions are similar to the light (A1) but you want to ride a larger motorcycle once qualified, then your age will make a difference as to which machine you can take your test on, and how soon you will be able to ride a larger machine.

Automatics

If you wish to take your test on a semi-automatic or a fully automatic machine, then you must bear in mind that you will only be able to ride this type of machine once qualified.

Applying for the standard (A) practical motorcycle test

Under 21

- The practical test must be taken on a machine over 120 cc but not exceeding 125 cc, and capable of 100 km per hour (approximately 62 mph).
- On passing, category A entitles you to ride a machine of up to 33.3 bhp (25 kw) or a power/weight ratio not exceeding 0.16 kw/kg, for a two-year restriction period.
- After this period you may ride any machine without having to take another test.
- If you reach the age of 21 before the end of your two-year probation period, and you want to ride a machine over the 33.3 bhp, you will be able to take the Accelerated Access Scheme (see Direct Access Scheme, page 84). If you pass you will be able to ride a machine of any size.

Over 21

You have the option of applying for the Direct Access Scheme (DAS) practical test on a machine of at least 46.6 bhp (35 kw). On passing the practical test, there is no restriction and you may ride a machine of any size.

Test documentation

CBT has largely remained the same, but has been revised in accordance with the changes in driving behaviour over the last few years (see Chapter 1). CBT Certificates are now valid for a three-year period from the date of issue. Prior to taking the test the DSA examiner will request to see your CBT Certificate, UK driving licence (with the correct entitlement), Theory Pass Certificate (if necessary) and photographic proof of identity (see page 126).

Direct/Accelerated Access Training

During Direct/Accelerated Access training you must by law wear fluorescent or reflective clothing and be

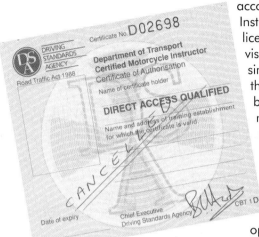

accompanied by a DAS Approved Instructor (request to see his or her blue licence) who must maintain radio and visual contact at all times. DAS is similar to that of training and taking the test on a 125 cc machine. You will be expected to ride according to the road and traffic conditions, that is, ride to the speed limit if safe to do so. However, larger machines have the potential to make better progress, particularly on national speed limits. You will be expected to make progress if you have the opportunity and it is safe to do so.

It is against the law for learner motorcyclists to ride a machine over 125 cc on the public roads without an approved DAS instructor.

Which course to choose

There are basically two types of training course available designed to get you to test standard and beyond.

Intensive training or block courses are the most popular. Depending on ability and experience, intensive courses usually consist of several days' training with the test on the final day. Usually the training scheme organizes everything, including the test, and in the event of failure most schemes offer 'unlimited training', so you only have to pay for another test and the use of the hire bike.

It is also possible to have hourly, or regular three-hour lessons, which are designed to get you to test standard over a period of time. Weekly lessons are beneficial to those who already own a vehicle, as it is possible to practise between lessons.

Whichever course you opt for, make sure that you inform your instructor of your previous riding experience. Even if you have had a ride on a friend's bike off-road, some experience is better than none. Be honest when relating past experience on the road. It is generally the responsibility of the instructor to find this information out; however, the more accurate you are, the more you will benefit from the training. If you have any doubts about which course to take, find out if your local training scheme will give you an assessment to establish your level of experience.

Hiring or buying a bike

Whether hiring or buying a bike, make sure that you are familiar with the basic checks (see Chapter 1, page 26). Carry out these checks even when returning to your machine after a short absence. If hiring a machine that looks like it has not had a clean for some time, make sure it is thoroughly checked. Often the smallest problems are spotted during cleaning. Some training schemes decide to invest in additional lubrication devices to improve performance and reliability. This is reassuring to know and might be the deciding factor when choosing which training scheme to go with. If you are unsure about the condition of your allocated machine, ask for another. Remember, you are the one who will be riding it!

Top Tips to Remember when Buying a Second-hand Motorcycle

- Arrive at least 10 minutes early so that you can hear the engine from cold.

- Check the frame and engine number against the numbers on the V5 registration document (log book).

- If the V5 document is photocopied or missing, it is advisable not to buy until completing an investigation.

- Ask to see receipts and old MOT certificates to check mileage and history of machine.

- Check wear of chain and sprockets, tyres, brake pads, exhaust, etc. If any are worn and need replacing, get a quote first before you buy.

- Always check that the electrics are in good working order.

- Find out if the machine has been dropped. Look for scratches, dents and broken or loose parts.

- Be aware that Q plate registrations are usually more expensive to insure. Find out why the vehicle was Q plated.

- It is advisable to get an insurance quote before you buy.

- If data-tagged or alarmed, the owner should be able to provide proof of purchase and the manufacturer's fitting certificate.

BACK TO BASICS

Machine familiarization – Direct Access Scheme

There are many benefits to riding a larger machine. Most people comment on the power difference and improved stability, particularly during higher speeds. General opinions conclude that the bigger machine gives you a smoother, more relaxed ride.

Larger machines will also have additional controls with which you will need to familiarize yourself. Make sure you understand all the controls and how they work before riding.

When moving on from riding a 125 cc to a 500 cc for example, most people have the tendency to believe that riding a larger machine will require more effort because it is bigger and heavier. In fact in most cases the opposite is true. Larger, modern machines require very little effort, and have been designed purposely for ease of use. Try to ride the machine from your wrists and ankles, and avoid making any sudden movements. So sit back and relax, let the machine do all the work!

Use of controls

Riding a larger machine requires more control, that is clutch and throttle control. Clutch control or 'riding the biting point' is required when pulling away and during slow manoeuvres, for example when turning in and out of junctions. Good use of clutch and throttle at slow speeds will also ensure a smooth and controlled manoeuvre.

Indelicate use of controls

This section should be named 'the worst that can happen', or common fears and experiences. For example, the fear (for some) of pulling a 'wheelie', moving forwards too quickly and out of control, pulling away in the wrong gear and stalling, losing balance and nearly dropping the machine at slow speeds, etc. There are some simple exercises that you can do to overcome these fears and improve your use of the controls. However, it is strongly advised that you have guidance from your approved DAS instructor.

Exercise 1: improving throttle control

- Start/warm the engine and look at the tachometer, more commonly known as the rev-counter.
- Turn the throttle and hold on a chosen point or number on the rev-counter. If your machine does not have a rev-counter turn the throttle and hold and remember the engine note that you have reached.
- Try this several times and listen to the sound of the engine. Once familiar with the sound, try again without looking, and then check to see if you have reached the same point.

Point to Remember

All machines have a point at which it is easier to hold the throttle steady. Finding this point on a larger, heavier machine will give the stability needed when attempting to pull away and riding slowly.

Exercise 2: avoiding panic reactions

This exercise is designed to reduce panic reactions to high-revving engines. Accidental twists of the throttle when you least expect it can sometimes break your concentration. Hopefully, if your clutch control is reasonably accurate you will find that although the engine is revving quite high, you will not bolt forwards.

- Pull away as you would normally.
- Slow down and continue to ride at a walking pace.
- Make sure you are comfortably 'riding the clutch on the biting point' and hold.
- When you have gained confidence and balance, increase the throttle and then release. Try to maintain the same speed by the use of the clutch.

Repeat the last part of this exercise several times.

Point to Remember

As long as you have a good hold on the 'biting point' you will be in control of your speed. Avoid turning the throttle quickly; learn to control the throttle using slow and gentle movements.

Slowing down and stopping

- Slowing down can be achieved either by the correct use of brakes, front and rear (see Chapter 1, page 39), or by 'engine braking', which is more noticeable on larger machines.
- Only use engine braking to regulate your speed when, for example, slowing down before a bend, proceeding downhill, following slow moving traffic, or riding on a slippery surface.

- Try not to rely on engine braking when slowing down to stop at traffic lights or give ways (unless on a bend). This is not good practice as you will find that you are only using your brakes at the end, which will make you unstable and give you a rough ride.
- Remember that the brakes are on the machine for a reason. Engine braking and changing down to slow down causes unnecessary wear on the engine. Stay in the gear suitable to the speed at which you are travelling.

Point to Remember

Gears are for going, brakes are for slowing.

Exercise 3: improving stability at slow speeds

Before starting this exercise it is important to be reminded of the movements during the application of the brakes. Walk forward with your machine and gently apply the front brake, cover the front brake and then gently squeeze the lever. If your machine dived and you felt that you nearly lost your balance, then you were probably too sharp when applying the front brake. Can you imagine what would happen if you were riding the machine slowly and applied the brake this hard? Now put the machine on the centre stand and spin the back wheel and apply the rear brake. Did you notice that there was very little movement from the application of this brake? The rear brake is a very useful one to use occasionally on its own during slow riding.

Practise the following:

- start/warm engine;
- pull away as you would normally;
- slow down and continue to ride at a walking pace;
- make sure you are comfortably 'riding the clutch on the biting point';
- hold clutch and throttle steady and apply and release rear brake gently.

Point to Remember

During slow riding, below 5 mph and turning, it is acceptable and safer to slow down and stop using the rear brake only. Always try to stop with steering straight.

Handling your machine

Top Tips When Handling Your Machine

- Avoid handling your machine on uneven surfaces.
- Keep the machine close to you – the bigger the gap, the less control you will have.
- Avoid turning the machine using 'full-lock'.
- Try parking your machine so that it is ready to drive out.
- Only use the centre stand on flat surfaces.
- Apply the front brake gently and only apply when upright and in a straight line.

ROAD JUNCTIONS

T-junctions

Although most junctions today are controlled by traffic lights, there are still many T-junctions that rely on the basic rules. Therefore, it is important to understand why we have give way markings at the end of some roads, and stop lines at others.

Give way markings are used to improve traffic flow. Generally, you are able to see the traffic flow before reaching the end of most give ways, enabling you to continue without stopping if is all clear (open junction).

You will usually find that when approaching a stop line you have little or no vision until you reach the line itself. Therefore, you must stop and have a proper look before you decide to go (closed junction).

It is not uncommon to approach the end of a give way and find that it is a closed junction. This is because of the changes to the environment over a period of time, including extensions to properties, increase in number of telephone boxes and bus stops, growth of trees and hedgerows and the increase of illegally parked vehicles.

Open junction

The rider approaches the end of the road and is able to see the traffic flow well before reaching the give way markings. The open junction enables the rider to maintain a steady speed without upsetting his or her balance.

Closed junction

- The rider can only see if there is anything coming when very close to the give way markings. Therefore, it is important to reduce speed and prepare to stop.
- After considering taking a lifesaver (LS) to the left to see if it is safe to turn (see Chapter 1) the rider finds it is easier and safer to look to the right at the end of the road (1).
- The rider establishes that it is safe to proceed, and looks into the road before moving into it (2).

Point to Remember

If approaching a stop line, you must stop at the line and then look to see if it is safe to proceed.

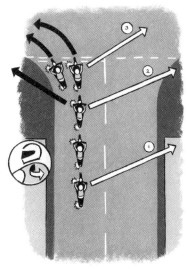

Turning left incorrectly

● This shows the rider observing too early (1) and not being able to see if there is anything coming.

● The rider has to look again (2) and in doing so has developed a poor position for the turn, which will force the rider into a slower, tighter turn. This position may also prompt another observation (3), which may upset the rider's balance.

● The rider is now forced into taking a lifesaver check too late, or in some cases not at all.

● The rider's position to the left would have made this manoeuvre much easier and safer, and is achieved by the correct timing of the first observation (between 1 and 2).

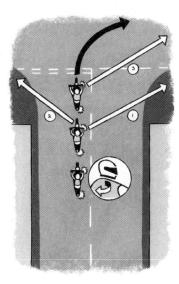

Turning right

● Turning right involves extra caution as you will have to negotiate and cross two streams of traffic.

● The rider considers taking a lifesaver check first (LS), and then looks to the right (1), then left (2) and finally right again (3), to establish that it is safe to proceed into the road before moving into it.

● If these observations are carefully timed in the order above, there should be no need for any extra observations if it is clear.

Parked cars and restricted vision

It is not uncommon to come across vehicles illegally parked within 10 metres of a junction in a built-up area.

- The rider can see between parked vehicles (1) before reaching the end of the road. However, by the time the rider approaches the give way markings the rider's vision is blocked (2).

- At this point it is necessary for the rider to continue forward to be able to see around the parked vehicles (3). The rider creates another junction and has imagined that the give way lines have moved to the edge of the parked vehicles.

- If it is safe to do so, this manoeuvre can be done without stopping at the original give way lines.

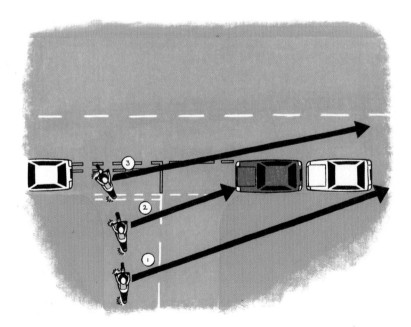

Stopping and giving way to traffic

- After considering a lifesaver check (LS), the rider looks to the right (1) and can see a vehicle that will prevent him or her from turning.

- After establishing that it is not safe to proceed, the rider concentrates on positioning the machine before the give way lines (2). Once in position, the rider looks to the right again (3) to establish a safe gap.

- If it looks like there will be no gaps for a while, take a look into the road that you want to move into (4) to establish whether it will be safe to do so and take this opportunity to look for any speed changes or hazards.

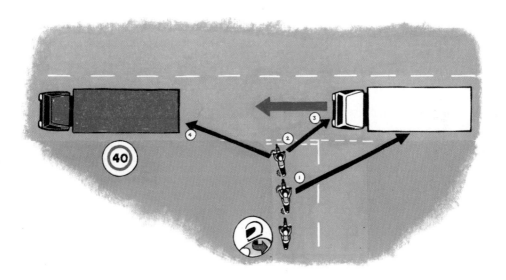

Crossroads and box junctions

Most crossroads today are controlled by traffic lights,
and have clear road markings to indicate positioning,
for example, when turning right. It is important to
remember that no two junctions are the same. Once
you understand the basic principles you should be
able to negotiate turning through any crossroad.

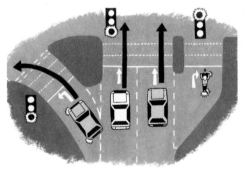

Traffic light-controlled crossroads

- The traffic lights control vehicles
  approaching the solid white stop line.
  Once past the stop line you do not
  have to adhere to the traffic lights.
  However, consider your safety when
  waiting to turn right. If the traffic
  lights change you may think that it is
  safer not to proceed through the
  junction. Think about your vulnerable
  position, particularly if a heavy goods
  vehicle were to turn into your road.

- A traffic light on 'green' means it is your turn to
  proceed through the junction. This does not neces-
  sarily mean that it is safe to do so. Emergency
  vehicles are able to travel through a red light, so
  always check left and right to be on the safe side.

- Some traffic light-controlled crossroads have 'filter' lights to clear the build-up of traffic turning right within the junction. You do not have to wait for the filter light to come on in order to proceed.

- Major crossroads are more likely to be controlled by filter systems. The normal green traffic light maybe replaced by a green arrow. Although this means that the oncoming traffic will have a red light, still make sure that it is safe to proceed.

Positioning when turning right

When approaching a crossroad your position to turn right will depend on who gets there first. If you are the first vehicle into the junction you will be able to choose the safest position to take, and other traffic must respond to this. If you have the situation whereby you approach at the same time as an oncoming vehicle intending to turn, one of you must decide where to stop, and the other must follow suit. There are two manoeuvres that can be used for turning right, although most traffic today tends to adopt and use the 'nearside-to-nearside' manoeuvre.

Turning nearside-to-nearside

- If there are no directional markings on the ground, it is important to adopt a safe and progressive position. This figure shows the rider positioned in the centre, allowing the oncoming vehicles to pass safely (1), and enabling traffic behind to continue ahead (2). This position will also allow the rider to see into the road that they are intending to turn into.

- The rider has adopted this position by using the centre lines (A and B) as a guide, the point where the two imaginary lines meet. This position enables the rider to move forward and turn.

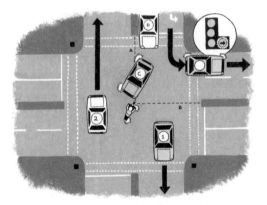

- Vehicle C's position is restricting the rider's vision. It would be unsafe for the rider to ease forward in this situation as vehicle D intends to continue straight on. Once vehicle C has completed the right turn, vehicle D will be able to proceed through the junction.

- The rider will have to wait until vehicle C has moved out of the way before deciding when it will be safe to go.

- The first figure on page 97 shows a similar manoeuvre. However, as there are specific right-turn filter lanes and arrows on the ground indicating the best position for the turn, the rider is able to move into position and see the flow of traffic safely.

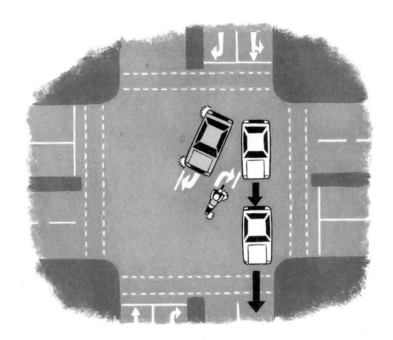

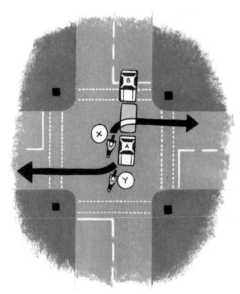

Turning offside-to-offside

Occasionally you may come across an oncoming vehicle ready to turn in the offside position (A). Rider X has moved forward and adopted a position behind vehicle (A). It is possible that other vehicles waiting to turn (B) may close the gap in which you have been forced into. If this is the case, you have no option but to wait until they have gone.

Rider Y has chosen the wrong position and will not be able to see and make progress through the junction.

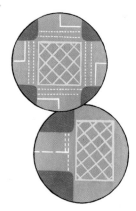

Understanding box junctions

A box junction is associated with yellow criss-cross lines within a yellow box, which are usually painted on the ground in the middle of a crossroad or just outside a busy junction.

'You must not enter a box junction unless your exit is clear. You may enter if you are turning right and are only prevented from doing so by oncoming traffic, and other vehicles waiting to turn right.' In order to understand this rule, it is important to remember the first part of the statement and always refer to it whichever direction you are turning.

Is your exit clear?

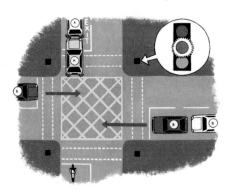

- The build-up of stationary traffic (A) prevents the rider from moving through and leaving the junction. The rider must keep the box junction clear and wait until the traffic ahead starts to move.

- It is important to keep your eye on the traffic lights while you are waiting to proceed. They could change to red, which means that the traffic queuing left and right (B) will eventually have a green light and will start to proceed. Hence the importance of keeping the junction clear.

- It is also important to remember to keep all pedestrian crossings clear for the same reason.

Turning right and applying the rule

'You must not enter a box junction unless your exit is clear. You may enter if you are turning right, if you are only prevented from doing so by oncoming traffic and other vehicles waiting to turn.'

- The rider has entered the box junction after checking that his or her exit is clear. A vehicle is already in the box junction and proceeds to turn.
- The vehicle's location in the box will not prevent the rider from moving into it, as they have both checked that their exit is clear. Consider your safety if the traffic lights change.
- As long as your exit is clear, you can queue up with other traffic waiting to turn right. However, remember to keep the pedestrian crossings clear, and consider your safety if the traffic lights change.

Point to Remember

Before you enter a box junction, make sure that your escape route, your exit, is clear.

● The figure on page 100 shows that the exit is blocked by a queue of stationary traffic (A). Rider X has stopped just outside the box, and is waiting for the traffic queue (A) to move before entering the box. Rider Y has kept the pedestrian crossing clear and has decided that it is safer to wait at the white stop line.

● Even if the traffic lights change to red, both riders will be in a safe position, clear from the flow of traffic. However, Rider X might restrict the movement of vehicles turning right into his or her road.

Roundabouts

Roundabouts are designed to keep traffic flowing and make it easier to complete the right-turn manoeuvre. There is one simple rule to be obeyed and that is to give priority to vehicles coming from the right. Remember to let traffic from the right pass safely before entering.

Priority to the right

Rider X is prevented from entering the roundabout due to vehicle A coming from the right. Rider Y is able to proceed onto the roundabout.

Turning left

As a rule, the first exit of the roundabout will be a left-turn procedure.

- In the figure above, the rider has approached the roundabout after completing a left-turn manoeuvre (see left and right turns, Chapter 1).
- The rider has established that it is safe and has joined the roundabout after considering a lifesaver check on the left (LS).

- Once on the roundabout, be aware of the traffic around you and what it is doing.
- Leaving the roundabout, the rider cancels the indicator and remains in the left-hand lane, as very often two lanes merge into one. It is possible that another vehicle might be overtaking.

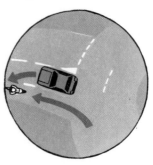

Straight ahead

As a rule, any exit after the first exit, and before the '12 o'clock' exit, will be treated as a straight ahead procedure.

It should not be necessary to indicate before entering a roundabout when continuing straight ahead. If you do indicate it might be confusing to other road users. It is also possible to use the middle or off-side lane, unless signs/arrows indicate otherwise, if the left-hand lane is congested with slow-moving vehicles.

- The rider has entered the roundabout after considering a lifesaver check to the left. Once on the roundabout, the rider approaches the exit on the left and continues looking for any traffic entering.
- The rider reaches the 'point of no return', the middle of the last exit before the one wanted, and signals left to let the other traffic know (B and C) that he or she is leaving the roundabout.

- The rider checks over the right shoulder to establish if it is safe to continue round to the right. There could be vehicles in the right-hand lane (A) taking the same exit. This observation should only take a split second, as the rider will have to keep checking on vehicle B.

- The rider cancels the indicator once the manoeuvre is completed.

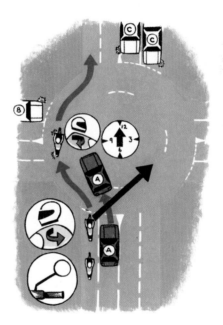

Right-turn manoeuvre

As a rule, anything past the 12 o'clock exit is classed as a right-turn manoeuvre. However, if you are continuing along a ring road and there are very few exits off the roundabout, you may consider it to be safer to proceed using a straight ahead manoeuvre.

- The rider has approached the roundabout after completing a right-turn manoeuvre (see left and right turns, Chapter 1).

- The rider has entered the roundabout after considering a lifesaver to the left (LS) to establish that the vehicle in the left lane (A) is not indicating right and not attempting the same manoeuvre, and that it is safe to proceed onto the roundabout. Vehicle A might attempt to straight-line the round-about, not leaving enough room for vehicles turning right.

- The rider approaches the island in the middle and slows down. It is important to adjust your speed before attempting to continue through a bend or curve.

- The rider continues, keeping close to the roundabout itself, as the rider is aware of other traffic on the left (vehicle C).

- The rider prepares to exit after passing the middle of the 12 o'clock exit and changes indication (left) and observes into the 12 o'clock exit in anticipation of vehicle D entering the roundabout before its turn.

- After checking that it is safe to leave the roundabout (LS), the rider concentrates on looking into the exit and leaving in a smooth, straight line.

Marked-up roundabouts

Marked-up roundabouts clearly indicate that you use and follow the lanes provided for your chosen desti-nation. You may also find abbreviated destinations painted within the lane. Marked-up roundabouts have been designed to improve lane discipline and reduce speed. Your first encounter with one of these round-abouts may be confusing. Comparing this type of roundabout with a normal one will make it easier to understand them.

- Turning right at a normal roundabout, that is a roundabout with no specific lanes and markings, is a simple and usually a quick manoeuvre.
- Rider X enters in a straight line, then follows the island in the middle closely and upon leaving changes indication and checks to see if it is safe before leaving in a straight line.
- Rider Y approaches a marked-up roundabout in the right lane provided. The rider enters the right lane on the roundabout and remains within this lane. Shortly after entering this lane, another arrow appears (either a straight-on arrow or in some cases a left-turn arrow).

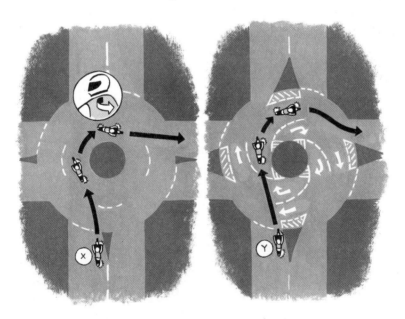

Understanding marked-up roundabouts

Looking at the same right-turn manoeuvre from a different perspective will make it easier to understand the importance of lane discipline.

- Rider X enters the normal roundabout and starts a right-turn manoeuvre.
- Vehicle A approaches and enters the same round-about before its turn as the rider prepares to exit.
- Vehicle A and the rider are now heading for a collision. Vehicle A might intend to take the 12 o'clock exit, which will prevent the rider from exiting and will cause the rider to slow down.
- Rider Y enters the marked-up roundabout and remains in the lane provided for his or her chosen exit.
- The rider completes the right-turn manoeuvre safely, without any interference from vehicle B.
- The lane markings have encouraged the rider to 'spiral-out', and have forced the rider to move closer to vehicle B, which now has no choice but to wait until the rider has exited.

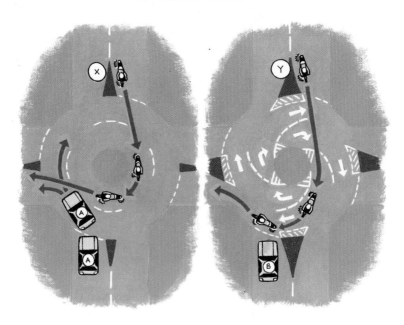

Point to Remember

Use marked-up roundabouts properly, as they have been designed for your safety. Take your time using these roundabouts. The faster you go the more likely it is that you will drift into another lane. Watch out for road users not using these roundabouts properly.

Mini-roundabouts

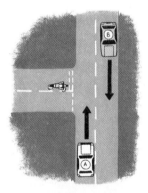

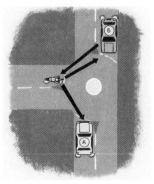

Mini-roundabouts should be dealt with in the same way as normal round-abouts. Mini-roundabouts have been created to slow traffic down and improve the traffic flow at awkward and busy T-junctions.

- The rider is waiting to turn out of the junction, but finds this difficult due to constant flow of traffic (vehicles A and B).

- A mini-roundabout is now in place where the rule 'priority to the right' applies. Although the rider has to give way to vehicle A, vehicle B has to slow down and give way to the rider.

Who has priority?

When approaching mini-roundabouts there is often confusion as to who has priority. It is often difficult to judge who goes first, particularly when you all arrive at the same time!

- The rider and vehicle A have arrived at the same time. At this point the rider has priority over vehicle A, and vehicle A has to give way to the rider.
- Vehicle B has not quite reached the give way lines and therefore does not affect the rider's decision. The rider can continue to turn left or right.
- If all three vehicles did arrive at precisely the same time, it is important that one of the three makes an instant decision. It is also possible to prevent this from happening if one of you is able to adjust your speed on approach, so that one of you arrives slightly later than the others, prompting a decision.

Indicating at mini-roundabouts

Indicating to turn left and right at a mini-roundabout is still necessary, as you need to inform other road users, which includes pedestrians, of your intention to change direction. However, it is not always possible to indicate when leaving a mini-roundabout or when continuing straight ahead.

- The rider has approached the mini-roundabout and intends to continue straight ahead. There are no other vehicles approaching the roundabout so the rider continues without indicating to exit.

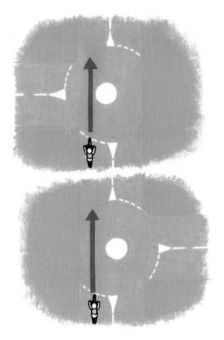

- The rider approaches the same mini-roundabout but this time there is an oncoming vehicle A, so the rider decides to indicate to exit so that vehicle A clearly understands where the rider is going.
- If the rider did not indicate, vehicle A might think that the rider was intending to turn right or complete a U-turn.

Understanding signposts

On the approach to most roundabouts you will see a signpost informing you of the destinations available at that roundabout. Once you have decided where you are going the natural course of action is to prepare for that manoeuvre. However, sometimes when you actually reach the roundabout itself you discover that what you saw on the board does not correspond with the layout of the roundabout.

The roundabout layout is different to the information given on the board. As a rule it is safer to go by the information on the signpost, as the lane markings on the roundabout will usually correspond with the information boards. However, there are always exceptions to the rule. If you have local knowledge and you feel it is safer to go by the roundabout layout rather than the information board, then do so.

Y-junctions

Y-junctions are usually located where a road ends on a bend. Their purpose is to improve vision and positioning, particularly when turning right. They also improve traffic flow, making it easier for vehicles to turn in and out of the junction, reducing the risk of an accident.

Y-junctions minor-to-major

- Rider A intends to turn left at the end of the road. The rider has chosen the correct route for this manoeuvre. Rider B has taken the incorrect route and will find it difficult to turn.

- Although rider C has had to deal with two junctions to complete a right-turn manoeuvre at the end of the road, the rider will have better vision and an easier turn than rider D.
- Major-to-minor, rider E takes the quickest route when turning left. Rider F will find it difficult to turn left.
- Rider G has chosen the correct position from which to turn right. Rider H will not only find it difficult to turn but will also have to deal with another junction.

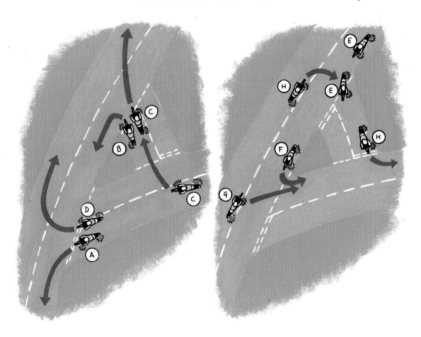

Staggered junctions

Two junctions close together can sometimes cause confusion as to who is going where and when. It is not uncommon to experience other drivers deliberately stopping short of their turn in order to let you out of your junction.

Approaching staggered junctions

- Vehicle A intends to turn right and has stopped short of the junction. Together with vehicle C they encourage vehicle B to proceed out of the junction.

- Although vehicles A, B and C seem to be communicating with each other, they fail to see the rider passing through.

- The rider and vehicle B could collide, as vehicle B has been distracted by vehicles A and C and has not anticipated the approach of any other vehicles.

Point to Remember

Be cautious when approaching staggered junctions in this way. Be aware of other vehicles communicating to each other and anticipate that they might not be aware of your presence.

Proceeding through staggered junctions

- The rider approaches the end of the road after completing a right-turn manoeuvre.

- After establishing that it is safe to proceed out of the junction, the rider changes indication as soon as possible to inform vehicle A of the intention to turn left.

- The rider finally checks that it is safe to turn after taking a lifesaver to the left.

ROAD SYSTEMS AND RULES

Types of road

Understanding the type of road you are on will help you determine the speed limit. Speed limits reflect the level of urbanization. Residential areas and places of intense activity tend to have reduced speed limits, usually 30 mph restrictions (and in some cases 20 mph). Out in the country where there is very little activity you usually have to comply with the national speed limit, which on a single carriageway is 60 mph, and 70 mph on dual carriageways.

Ring roads can be found circling most towns and cities. Their purpose is to increase traffic flow and divert heavy volumes of traffic away from the city centres. Ring roads can be a mixture of both single and dual carriageways, and usually have higher speed restrictions.

Identifying speed limits

There are three general rules with regard to speed limits:

- in a built-up, lit area and where there are no speed limit signs, the speed limit will be 30 mph;
- in the country, where there are very few buildings and no street lighting, you must not exceed the national speed limit, which is 60 mph on a single carriageway;
- most speed changes occur at junctions, roundabouts and before entering and leaving residential areas.

Built-up areas

It is not uncommon to travel along a 40 mph road and not see any speed signs reminding you that you are in a 40 mph speed limit area. Signs are not always visible, particularly during the summer months, and it could be that they are missing, blown down or even turned around. It is possible to establish roughly what the speed limit is even without a speed sign.

As a guide

- You are travelling along a 40 mph road but there are no visible signs reminding you of the speed limit. The road could be 30 mph or 40 mph, as the area is built up.
- Look for a road leading into a residential area, either a turning on the left or right. Look into this road and if you see a 30 mph sign it is reminding you to slow down before entering the residential area.
- Therefore, the road you are on is likely to have a higher speed limit.

If you are travelling along a 30 mph road, and wish to leave the road you are on and enter a residential area, you should not see any speed restriction signs when turning into that road, confirming that the road you just left was a 30 mph limit.

Point to Remember

There are always exceptions to every rule: you could be travelling along a 30 mph road and still see 30 mph signs on entrances to side roads. It is easier to identify speed changes as soon as they occur, usually at junctions.

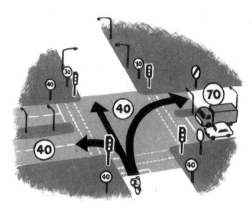

Speed changes at crossroads

- The rider waits at the traffic lights and can clearly see all the speed changes.

- Turning left, the rider enters a 40 mph limit.

- Turning right, the rider prepares to build speed up to 70 mph.

- Straight ahead the road continues as a 30 mph limit.

Road markings

Most road markings are fairly straightforward. However, diagonal stripes or chevrons, which are usually found at junctions and in the centre of the road, can cause some confusion:

- you may enter or cross a broken line if it is safe to do so;

- you must *not* cross or straddle a solid or unbroken line unless:
  - entering premises or a side road;
  - overtaking a stationary vehicle, a road maintenance vehicle, pedal cycle or a horse being ridden or led at a speed not exceeding 10 mph;
  - directed to do so by a police officer or a traffic warden;
  - in an emergency situation.

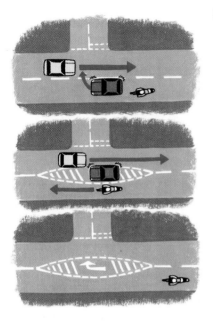

Understanding broken lines and chevrons

- Before chevrons are in place, a vehicle has taken up a position to turn right and is prevented from turning due to an oncoming vehicle.

- The rider is also prevented from making progress due to the position of the vehicle in front.

- With the chevrons in place, the vehicle turning right has a designated area to move into, allowing vehicles to pass safely either side. The vehicle in the middle is also in a safe area for turning right.

- It is not uncommon to find chevron areas with arrows encouraging road users to enter.

> **Point to Remember**
>
> Chevrons are used to separate traffic and protect vehicles turning right.

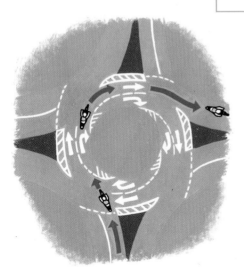

Solid lines and chevrons

- The rider has entered the round-about in the right-hand lane and then proceeds straight ahead, remaining in the lane provided.

- The rider is aware of the solid chevron areas which have been placed to guide the rider safely into the exit.

- The rider must not cross or straddle the solid lines, and therefore must slow down to avoid this happening.

Approaching priority systems

Priority systems are usually in place to control the traffic flow through narrow junctions, although more recently they have been used as a form of traffic calming. It is important when approaching a priority system to establish who has priority. It is also important to remember that the signs only affect those approaching the system on the road where the signs are located.

Priority systems

- The rider approaches the end of the road (A) and intends to turn left.
- Until the rider enters road B, the rider does not have priority over the oncoming traffic.
- It is safer for the rider to wait at the end of road A until the vehicle has passed him or her by. On entering road B the rider will have priority over any oncoming traffic.

Understanding pedestrian crossings

There are several types of pedestrian crossing: zebra, pelican, puffin, toucan and controlled crossing. There are also rules to be obeyed when approaching all of the above with or without zigzag lines:

- you must keep crossings clear at all times;
- you must not park on a crossing;
- you must not overtake before a crossing. When on a dual carriageway, you must not overtake the leading vehicle into the crossing;
- pedestrians must not cross within the zigzag lines.

Zebra crossings

Zebra crossings that are located close to junctions or on a wide road are usually divided by islands. Zebra crossings that are divided like this can be treated as two separate crossings:

- The rider approaches a zebra crossing that is divided by an island.
- The oncoming vehicle prepares to stop to allow the pedestrian to cross.
- The rider proceeds through the crossing as the pedestrian has not reached the island.
- If the crossing does not have an island it becomes one crossing, and you must stop and wait until the crossing is clear.

Pelican crossings

Pelican crossings are traffic light-controlled. The traffic light sequence is slightly different to a normal set of traffic lights:

- Although the red light has now changed to flashing amber, the rider waits patiently for the pedestrian to reach the other side of the road safely before moving off.
- If there are no pedestrians crossing and the amber light is flashing, you may proceed if it is safe to do so.
- If the crossing is staggered treat it as two separate crossings.

Puffin and toucan crossings

Puffin and toucan crossings are both traffic light-controlled and are very similar to the original pelican crossing. Both crossings have sensors fitted so that when a pedestrian approaches the crossing the sensor activates the traffic light. Unlike the pelican crossing, the puffin and toucan crossing use the normal traffic light sequence. Toucan crossings refer to the fact that 'two can cross' at the same time. That is, both pedestrians and cyclists. A toucan crossing will have a green cyclist lit at the same time as the familiar 'green person'.

Identifying cycle lanes and advanced stop lines

Cycle lanes are marked by solid or broken white lines on the road. You may also find a blue information sign displaying a white cycle at the beginning of the cycle lane. Some cycle lanes are only operational during certain times during the day. Look out for any time plates indicating these times.

Advanced stop line

- At present, cycle lanes and advanced stop lines can only be used by pedal cyclists, unless they state otherwise.
- The pedal cyclist has reached the furthest white stop line. The rider has stopped at the first white stop line.
- The cyclist is now in an advanced position to be able to get a head start.

Point to Remember

It is important that all road users anticipate cyclists riding on the inside with or without cycle lanes.

Dealing with level crossings and tramways

Crossing railway lines and tram lines in the wet can be hazardous. It is particularly important that you avoid excessive acceleration, braking or leaning. If following a vehicle through a crossing or over tram lines you must maintain a safe distance. When riding over tram lines try to avoid getting your wheels caught in the grooves, as this will make it difficult to steer your machine.

One-way streets

Due to the increase in vehicles on the road over the years, there is generally less space on the road for parking. Parking is particularly a problem within inner city areas. In some cases the roads are so congested with parked vehicles that it is almost impossible for two cars to pass each other safely. The solution to this

problem has been to turn these types of roads into one-way streets.

Three steps to converting a road into a one-way street:

- introduce several one-way traffic signs along the road;
- change the road markings at both ends of the road;
- place two no entry signs at the end of the road.

Identifying one-way streets

- If a road has been converted into a one-way street it is sometimes difficult to identify that it is a one-way, and can be confusing when turning right.
- The rider intends to turn right at the end of the road.
- The rider reaches the end of the road and has failed to identify any one-way signs.
- The rider observes that there is a dividing line and is led to believe that the road is two-way.
- Although the road appears to be normal the rider has failed to spot the double dotted give way lines and how they both continue to the other side of the road.

- The rider should be positioned on the right side of the road for this manoeuvre.
- A road that has been specifically made to be a one-way is very easy to identify.

Riding through fords

A ford is where a stream crosses a road. The time of year will affect how deep the stream will be. You will often find a measuring stick within the stream so that you can identify whether it is safe to proceed through it. Riding through a ford will affect your machine in several ways:

- If your exhaust is below the water line then you must keep the engine running quite high so that the water is unable to enter the exhaust and flood the engine.
- If you are unable to see to the bottom you must anticipate a bumpy ride. Deep, faster-flowing streams will often carry and deposit stones, boulders and household rubbish.
- Travelling too quickly through a ford may cause you to aquaplane and lose control. It is safer to ride through at a steady, constant speed to maintain traction. (Ride through at the highest point of the road – usually the centre.)
- Once safely through a ford your brakes will be wet and less effective. It is vital that you try and test your brakes safely as soon as possible.

Bus lanes

Bus lanes can usually be found on major roads in and out of towns and cities. Bus lanes can either be used permanently by buses or operational only during peak times. If heading into town you can expect a bus lane to be operational during the morning rush hour, eg, Monday to Friday between the hours of 7.30 am and 9.30 am. Leaving the town or city you would expect the bus lane to be in operation Monday to Friday between the hours of 4.00 pm and 6.00 pm. Times and days do vary so make sure you know what day and time it is before you make your decision. Bus lanes can also be used by cyclists, motorcyclists and taxis if the sign includes a picture of them.

Understanding bus lanes

- The rider approaches a bus lane and identifies a time plate indicating that the bus lane is operational and in use Monday to Friday between the hours of 7.30 am and 9.30 am.
- The rider has checked the time and realizes that it is 9.45 am.
- The rider uses the bus lane as it is not in operation.

End of bus lane

- The rider is not using the bus lane as it can only be used by buses.

- The rider approaches the end of the bus lane and intends to continue straight ahead.

- The lane the rider is currently in becomes a right-turn-only lane.

- The rider must merge into the left-hand lane to continue straight ahead.

- The rider looks for the 'end of bus lane' sign, as he or she knows that you must not rely on the arrows on the ground as they could be indicating a side turning.

- It is also possible that he or she may not be able to see the arrows due to volume of traffic.

- The rider recognizes that the queue of traffic in the left-hand lane is backing into the bus lane.

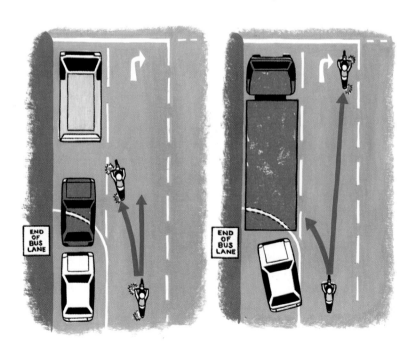

- The vehicles in the bus lane are breaking the law so it is important that you know where the bus lane ends.
- The rider now has two options. Once past the 'end of bus lane' sign the rider may be able to wait ready to merge with the traffic if it is safe to do so, or continue in the right-hand lane and turn right.

TEST DAY

Most training schemes will offer a pre-test lesson as part of block or intensive training. This usually consists of a one-hour lesson which is just enough riding before your test. The instructor should get you to the test centre 10 minutes prior to the test. This will give you the opportunity to relax, prepare your documents and familiarize yourself with the test centre.

The test centre

There is usually a designated parking area for motorcycles. You should park your vehicle ready to drive out to make it easier for you when the moment arrives. The examiner will expect to find you in the waiting-room with your documents in hand. Remember, the examiner has not got the time to play hide and seek!

Your test machine

The examiner will not expect you to check your machine before the test. This must be done before you arrive at the test centre. The examiner will check the machine for roadworthiness, and will also look for a valid tax disc, legal tread depth and that the 'L' plates are clearly displayed front and rear.

Checking your documents

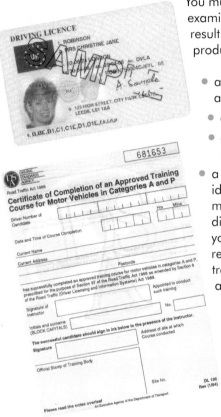

You must show certain documents to the examiner before the test. Failure to do so will result in your test being terminated. You must produce:

- an appropriate, valid driving licence with the appropriate motorcycle or moped category;
- a CBT certificate (DL196);
- a moped/motorcycle Theory Pass Certificate (provisional licence holders only);
- a form of photographic proof of your identity, for example your passport. You must be able to produce a document that displays a recent photograph of you, and your signature. As a last resort supply a recent passport photograph and your training scheme will be able to provide the appropriate document.

The eyesight check

If you need glasses to read a number plate you must wear them while riding on the road and during your test. You will be required to read a number plate at a distance of 20.5 metres (67 feet approximately), with letters 79.4 millimetres high. If you fail to read the number correctly the examiner will terminate the test and you will lose your test fee. You will be able to book another test straight away. Give yourself time to visit the optician!

The practical accompanied motorcycle test

The motorcycle test will last up to 42 minutes from the moment the examiner calls your name. This includes:

- checking your documents;
- signing against your name to say that the vehicle you are riding is insured;
- fitting the intercom;
- checking your eyesight;
- checking your machine for roadworthiness;
- the test itself;
- end of test questions;
- issuing the appropriate document at the end.

During the test itself the examiner will give you clear and early directions. If the examiner does not say anything you must continue straight ahead. If the examiner asks you to take the next available turning on the left or the right, remember to look out for 'no entry' signs.

Try not to be preoccupied with what the examiner is doing. Try to forget that the examiner is behind you. It is possible during your test to pass through a junction when the traffic lights change. The examiner may have to stop at the traffic lights, and depending on how long the examiner is kept waiting you may be asked to pull over. If the examiner does not say anything you must continue riding according to the road and traffic conditions.

Test exercises

You will be asked to carry out various exercises, which may include:

- an emergency stop;
- putting the machine on a stand;
- pushing the machine round to the other side of the road;
- riding the machine round completing a U-turn;
- an angled start;
- slow riding;
- a hill start.

The examiner will find a quiet residential area to conduct most or all of the above exercises. He or she will send you off on your own around the block before the emergency stop. The examiner will not expect you to stop if there is a vehicle behind you. If this is the case, the examiner will ask you to continue around the block again. After completing the emergency stop you must pull over to the left, as quickly and as safely as possible. You do not have to wait for the examiner to instruct you to do this.

End of test questions

You will be asked a question at the end of the test about carrying a pillion passenger. Common questions include:

- *What should your pillion passenger consider with regard to safety equipment and clothing?*
  The passenger should wear an approved safety helmet, which fits properly and is securely fastened. The passenger should wear clothing that is protective, comfortable and will keep him or her warm and dry.

- *How should a pillion passenger sit on the back of your machine?*
  Sitting astride the machine, facing forwards with feet on the footrests, holding on suitably. Whilst riding stay parallel with machine and rider. Keep out of rider's view when he or she is looking back.

- *How will a pillion passenger affect your riding?*
  Carrying a pillion will affect your balance while under acceleration, braking and cornering. The steering will feel lighter during acceleration, heavier under braking and less responsive while cornering.

- *Will you be able to slow down and stop the same as when you are on your own?*
  It may take longer to stop in an emergency, so it is important to consider doubling your braking distance.

- *What should you adjust on your machine before carrying a pillion?*
  Suspension, tyre pressures, possibly headlights and mirrors.

- *How would you advise a pillion to carry out arm signals?*

    It is not advisable for a pillion to do arm signals.

- *If carrying luggage or shopping, what must you check before riding off?*

    That the luggage is evenly distributed, secure and not exceeding the maximum weight allowance for the machine.

The result

After you have answered the questions you will be told whether you have passed or failed. If you have passed, the examiner will request to see your driving licence again and will complete your test pass certificate.

Upon passing the motorcycle test you will be able to:

- apply for your full motorcycle category. You must send your test pass certificate along with your driving licence and an administration fee to the DVLA. If not added to your licence within two years of passing your test you must take the test again;
- ride without 'L' plates on your own;
- take a pillion passenger;
- ride on motorways.

You may accumulate up to 15 minor faults during the test and still pass. However, sometimes the accumulation of the same minor fault can turn into a serious fault. One serious or dangerous fault will result in failure. If you have failed, you will be given a driving test report showing the areas you failed on. There is usually a waiting period before being allowed to re-apply for another test. If you have not failed, but have not completed the test, you do not have to wait to re-apply for another test.

It is also possible that your test may be cancelled or terminated due to bad weather, a fault or a problem concerning the examiner's machine, or an administrative error. If you have any doubts about your test check with your training scheme or ring the driving test centre. You will find these details on your test appointment card.

If your test is cancelled by the DSA, you will be refunded or reallocated a new test date.

PART THREE

ADVANCED RIDING

ADVANCED RIDING

This chapter explains techniques that will teach you to negotiate hazards with confidence at the correct speed, reducing the chance of things going wrong. Basically, advanced riding takes away the element of luck that a lot of riders seem to depend on. If every road user had a bit more consideration for others using the road, there would be fewer accidents and virtually no such thing as road-rage.

AIMS OF AN ADVANCED RIDER

'Why bother? I know how to ride a bike! Advanced riding is just for coppers and armchair experts.'

Wrong! Advanced riding takes great skill and is a technique that once learnt and practised will not only make you a safer rider, but will ensure you get the most out of the machine you are riding, whether it be a race-rep or a large tourer.

The aim of an advanced rider 'is to be capable of making maximum progress safely and without inconvenience to other road users'.

So what does it mean? To begin with, it does not mean jumping onto a motorbike and riding it as fast as you can in a straight line along the public highway. Any idiot can do that. It also means that speed is only unsafe if used at the wrong time and in the wrong place. Knowing and using the Highway Code will also ensure you get your speed right.

HAZARDS

What then, is a hazard? A hazard is anything that is or could be a danger to you. For example, a car pulling out of a side road in front of you. A bend has potential danger, as there could be something around the bend that is out of sight. The road surface could be slippery, or your speed could be too fast for the conditions of the road.

The main categories of hazards are:

- physical, such as junctions, bends, brow of a hill, roundabouts, other road users, etc;
- weather conditions – rain, ice, fog, bright sunlight;
- the time of day;
- road conditions, poor surfaces, painted markings, drains and inspection covers and so on.

CONCENTRATION, OBSERVATION, POSITION, PLANNING AND SPEED (COPPS)

The basic principle of COPPS is described under the following headings: concentration, observation, position, planning and speed.

Concentration

You must be able to concentrate on what you are doing to achieve the best results. We all have the ability to concentrate, but the length that we can maintain it will vary. Therefore you must increase the ability to recognize when you are losing concentration, so that you can regain it. The longer you ride the shorter the time between maximum concentration and not concentrating. If you are finding it difficult to concentrate for more than 10 minutes, stop for a break.

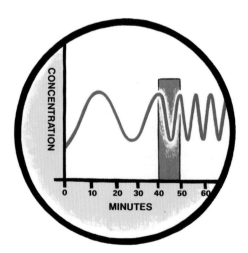

Observation

This means being able to look at something, register in your mind what you have seen and act on it. You need to develop the ability to be able to scan both ahead and behind and observe the things that will help make your ride smoother and safer. For example:

- a road sign informing you of a bend to the right (offside), or a slow-moving vehicle. Both require some form of action. Thinking about what you have seen, you also need to consider what you cannot see and also what you can reasonably expect to develop.

- There is a high-sided vehicle coming towards you. You are unable to see what is immediately behind it, but there could be another vehicle that may then suddenly overtake. Use your mirrors constantly, as these will give you an accurate picture of what is going on behind you.

Point to Remember

If necessary, consider a rear observation, but remember 90 per cent of the time you should be looking forward and only 10 per cent behind.

Position

Once you have taken into account everything that you have observed you can proceed to take up the safest position on the road. The safest position on the road can vary depending on whether there are any immediate hazards. There is not a right or wrong position. For example, consider the following:

- Riding along a straight road with no immediate hazards or dangers. You could safely travel anywhere on that road.

- Add a hazard such as an oncoming car. It would be safer to move away from the danger, to the left (nearside).

- Add a junction on the nearside, and if we can see well into the junction and it is clear, the greatest danger is still the moving oncoming car.

- However, if your view into the junction is obscured, it would be dangerous to move to the nearside. Still considering the danger of the oncoming car it would also be dangerous to move closer to the centre. If you experience conflicting dangers, one on the left and one on the right, you must consider slowing down.

- Add a fast-moving vehicle coming up behind you. You still need to consider a safe position for the hazards ahead, but the vehicle behind will determine when and how soon you obtain a safe position. You should not cause another vehicle to alter course or speed, so you may need to alter your own position and speed.

Planning

If you have observed the road ahead accurately you will have adopted the safest position on the road. This position should give you the best possible view of the road ahead without putting yourself in any danger, and without being a danger to other road users. From this position you can plan your next move. For example:

- You have taken up a position to the nearside on the approach to a blind right-hand bend.

- As you approach the apex of the bend and once the bend opens up, you can plan your position for the next stretch of road.

- If the road continues to take a course to the right, your position will remain the same, unless there are any other dangers that conflict with this position.

- If the road changes course, you should consider changing your position so that you increase your range of vision.

> ### Point to Remember
>
> If there are no other conflicting hazards or dangers, your position on the road will be determined by which way the road is taking you. From this position you will be able to plan the safest route through that stretch of road.

Speed

You need to have considered all of the above before making a decision to increase your speed. If you have not considered all of the above, you must slow down.

CORNERING

Cornering is one of the most exciting aspects of motor-cycling, and to be a good and safe rider it must be mastered correctly.

Tightness of a bend

On approaching a corner you should be looking for the arrowhead. This is an optical illusion and like the 'mind's eye' three-dimensional pictures, you have to train to see this clearly. It is basically where the two sides of the road appear to come together to form an arrowhead. This can be called the 'limit point' or 'vanishing point' and depending on what is happening to this point depends on the actions you must take. When the arrowhead is stationary, the bend is tight and you will possibly need to change your speed and position. When the arrowhead appears to be moving away from you, you are in the correct position and travelling at the correct speed. Practising at lower speeds to begin with will help improve your judgement.

Left-hand bend

When approaching a left-hand bend the best position to be in is towards the offside of the road, bearing in mind offside dangers such as oncoming vehicles and junctions. If there are no oncoming vehicles and the road is clear, you could consider using the whole width of the road. This would then give you a better view into the bend. If the limit point is now moving away from you, the bend is less severe due to your new position and speed can be maintained. This may not be done if it means crossing or straddling a solid white line, or committing a moving traffic offence, or if by your movements you cause other road users inconvenience or confusion.

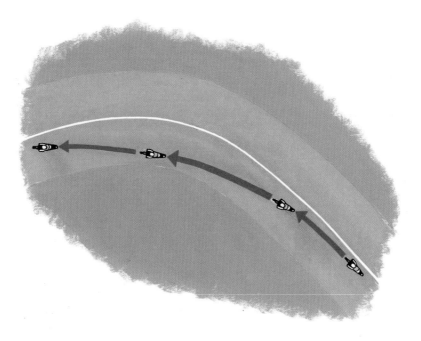

Right-hand bend

When approaching a right-hand bend the best position is to be towards the nearside of the road, bearing in mind nearside dangers such as drains, pedestrians, nearside junctions, parked vehicles and debris that could have been pushed to the side of the road.

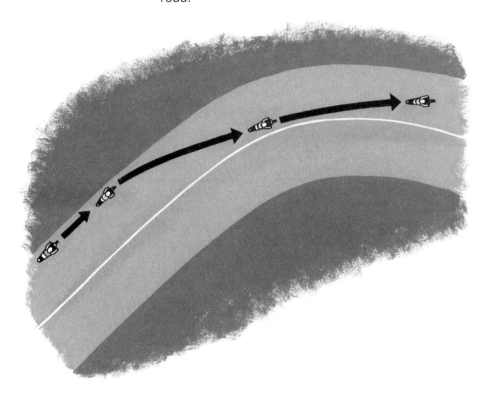

Following a high-sided vehicle

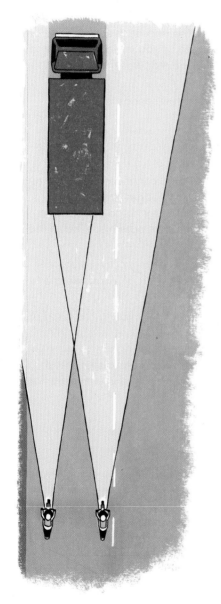

This will change your position. For example:

- By holding further back from the vehicle, you will be able to get a view down the nearside or offside by moving slightly to the left or right. You will also find that when approaching a bend by holding your position, you can maintain your view.

- Approaching a left-hand bend. Usually we would position to the offside to open up the view into the bend. If we do this too soon, the high sides of the vehicle we are following will block our view. Therefore by staying over to the nearside until the lead vehicle is almost at the bend and then moving across to the offside gradually, our forward observation will be maintained. When the vehicle is ascending or descending a hill, by holding back you should be able to look over the top to see the road ahead.

Principles of cornering

- Plan well ahead.
- Ease off the throttle on the approach so that you can gently increase the speed as you negotiate the bend, which in turn will settle the rear wheel throughout the manoeuvre.
- Practise the technique at low speeds to ensure smoothness at high speed.

Things to consider:

- Can you see where the road continues? Scan left and right, look through gaps in hedges, trees, buildings, etc. Like a game of snooker, try not to plan for the first shot, plan as far ahead as possible. What is the road surface like?
- Can you take the bend in a straight line safely and lawfully without being confusing or inconsiderate to other road users?
- Is your machine capable of negotiating this bend at this speed?

Remember, bends are fun, but a motorcycle is most stable in an upright position travelling in a straight line.

OVERTAKING

Overtaking is one of the most dangerous manoeuvres a motorcyclist will do. If you never overtake, your riding will be very safe but you will miss out on the sense of achievement of an overtake, and you could certainly never class yourself as an advanced rider, as the aim of an advanced rider is 'to be capable of making maximum progress safely and without inconvenience to other road users'.

Main principles of overtaking

What is the speed of the vehicle you are about to overtake? What is the speed and performance of your bike? What is the approaching speed of any vehicles coming towards you, either in view or that could come into view?

Bearing these questions in mind, the question you should now ask is, 'Can I overtake and safely make the nearside, without causing any other road user to alter course or speed?'

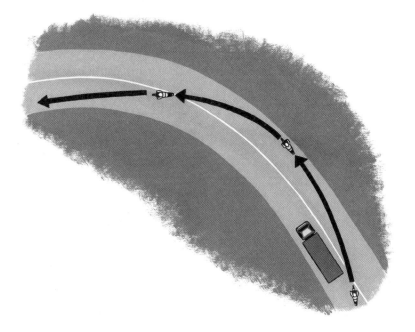

Things to consider:

- If you are following a line of vehicles, how close are they travelling to each other? You may find that the gaps are relatively small, so you may have to shorten the distance you overtake to give you more time to come back in between other vehicles. A safe train of thought is, 'If I can overtake three, I'll overtake two.' This way you will always have that safety margin.

- During the overtake, your position should open up the view ahead. Consider the above principles. If you then find you can safely extend the overtake, continue.

Point to Remember

If you are overtaking and you are approaching a left-hand bend, you are now in a better position to see through the bend, but bear in mind that you must have considered all the points we have mentioned in the cornering section.

If you have a high-sided vehicle coming towards you, before you overtake make sure you know what is behind it. This may mean moving into the nearside. This not only gives you a better view of the oncoming high-sided vehicle, but if you abort the overtake, it gives better protection from buffeting when the vehicle passes you.

If in doubt, do not overtake!

BRAKING

When you first learnt to ride a motorbike, you should have been taught that the front brake is the main stopping force, and in most circumstances you must apply the front before the rear. However, there are times when we should consider not using it.

There are two main ways in which we can lose speed:
1) By deceleration, closing the throttle and letting friction and engine compression slow the machine; and
2) By applying the brakes.

Brakes must always be applied, not grabbed, even in an emergency situation. As soon as the brakes are applied you are taking the momentum force away. But it does not just disappear – it has to go somewhere and it usually goes sideways. With good quality tyres and correct suspension settings, you will brake more effectively. You could have the best brake pads and disks in the world but if your tyres are badly worn you will find it hard to control during even the lightest braking.

Your aim should be to bring the bike to a smooth stop without locking either wheel. The brakes are at their most efficient just prior to locking up. There should not be any excessive fork dive or unbalance.

To achieve this we return again to the principles of COPPS.

When not to use the front brake first

As you are aware, all braking should be done when travelling in a straight line, and when the machine is in an upright position. But there will be occasions, for example when travelling over very slippery surfaces, or during a bend, where the application of the front brake would cause the bike to slide to one side. The best course of action is to apply the rear brake and, if further braking is necessary, gently apply the front.

Remember as a general guide:

- brake when travelling upright in a straight line;
- use the front before the rear brake;
- brake in plenty of time;

- be aware of the road surface and vary brake pressure accordingly;
- never grab, always apply the brakes.

For braking distances and an explanation of thinking distance, refer to *The Highway Code*.

CHANGING GEAR

To be an advanced rider, you must be able to know when a gear change is necessary and complete it smoothly.

When asked why we need to change gear I use the analogy of riding a pedal cycle. Your legs are the pistons driving the crank round that turns the rear drive wheel. When moving off from a standing start, we need minimum resistance or else we would have to use unnecessary energy to power the wheel around. To achieve this we start in a low gear, or the largest cog, ie, first gear. As we move off down the road the speed of the cycle becomes too fast for our legs to keep up with so we change to a higher gear. Again, once the speed becomes too great we change up once more, and so on until we meet a greater resistance such as a hill. Then the speed drops and we need to change down to a lower gear to reduce the resistance.

A motorbike is exactly the same – if the resistance becomes too great for the gear we are in, the bike will stall, or if we do not change gear we cannot increase speed.

Points to remember when changing gear:

- Have I achieved the right speed for this gear?
- When approaching a hazard, will this gear allow me the flexibility to accelerate or decelerate safely to negotiate the hazard?

- Have I taken enough speed off to change to a lower gear?

Common faults include:

- staying too long in a low gear, straining the engine and over-revving;
- staying too long in a high gear and labouring the engine. Remember how your legs would feel!;
- missing a gear, not engaging the gear properly due to a rushed clutch and throttle action;
- late gear changing due to poor observations or poor assessment of hazards;
- using the gears as brakes, unless the road surface is slippery and there could be a chance of skidding.

SKIDDING

There is nothing more disconcerting than a motorcycle skidding. A skid occurs when one or both of the wheels lose their grip on the road surface. The forces acting on the bike become greater than the tyres' traction with the road.

A motorcycle is most stable when travelling in a straight line in an upright position. The forces acting on the bike are limited to gravity and friction, keeping the tyres on the road and momentum driving the bike forward. As soon as you start to lean or turn a bike, other forces start to apply: centrifugal force, which acts in the opposite direction to the way the machine is leaning or turning, ie, trying to keep the bike upright, and reactionary force, which is the direction the bike will want to travel due to the pull of gravity and centrifugal force.

Types of skid

There are two types of skid: front wheel and rear wheel. The hardest to control is the former as it happens so quickly that it is hard to detect and react fast enough to counter it.

The main causes of skid are excessive acceleration, excessive leaning and breaking too hard.

The only way to come out of a skid safely is to remove the cause. For example, if when negotiating a left-hand bend the bike starts to skid to the right, remove the cause, bring the bike upright and reduce speed until control has been regained, then continue to negotiate the bend. Virtually all skids can be avoided with good observations and anticipation using the COPPS method of riding. . .

Look for warning signs, for example the weather conditions; the type of hazard, ie, corners and roundabouts are more likely to have diesel spillages; road surface; your own tyre condition.

Aquaplaning

This occurs when riding too fast over poorly drained roads covered in water. It is more likely to occur if your tyres are worn. The basic principles to remember are:

- slow down;
- stay upright;
- once through the water, gently apply your brakes to dry them off;
- when riding through deep water, engage first gear, keep the revs up by slipping the clutch and try not to cause waves.

ACCELERATION

As an advanced rider it is important to know how your machine responds to acceleration, and how quickly it will accelerate. Acceleration sense is the ability to increase or decrease the speed of your bike to match the existing road or traffic conditions by accurate use of the throttle. This can be of benefit in several ways:

- On the approach to a parked car, by easing off slightly on the throttle you give an oncoming car time to pass and then gently open the throttle to safely negotiate the parked vehicle. This reduces the need to change gear or brake, so you have taken less time to negotiate the hazard and reduced the chance of skidding.
- While overtaking a line of moving vehicles, easing off the throttle slightly enables you to move smoothly between them and so match the lead vehicle's speed and not cause the vehicle following to brake.
- When coming up behind a slower moving vehicle, judging the speed and matching it with acceleration sense rather than leaving it late, having to brake and then using harsh acceleration to overtake.
- On the approach to a bend, easing off slightly rather than braking, which allows the corner to be negotiated smoothly.

Types of acceleration

- Delicate – when on loose, slippery or uneven surfaces.
- Normal – when the machine is upright and travelling in a straight line on a good surface.
- Firm – when necessary to leave a hazard quickly or to complete an overtake safely in a straight line and on good surfaces.

Of course, this kind of judgement, along with all the advice found in this book, is made possible by using COPPS.

OBSERVATION LINKS

This is when we play detective. Observation links play a very important role in the planning part of COPPS, although we must bear in mind that what we think is likely to happen may not always be the case. For example, you are travelling in the country, and in the distance over the hedgerow you see a solitary lamppost. You should consider that this lamppost is there for a reason and could be illuminating some kind of danger. This is usually a junction or telephone kiosk, etc.

You see a high-sided vehicle in the distance to your offside, travelling at a right angle to you. You should question the angle and consider that the high-sided vehicle is either emerging from a junction, or that the road bends to the right.

A church spire in the distance highlights the fact that you are approaching a village or town.

A circle of lampposts highlights some form of junction or roundabout.

Fresh mud on the road could mean that you may come across cattle or slow-moving farm machinery.

Noticing a bus stopping or stationary should make you anticipate and look out for pedestrians running out from behind it.

Pedestrian lights or traffic lights on green can only change to red.

On motorways or dual carriageways, watch the vehicle you intend to overtake. Is it gaining on the vehicle ahead? Are its wheels getting closer to the white carriageway markings? Has the driver checked his or her rear view mirrors?

There are endless things you can use to help you plan the safest course of action. With practice they will become a natural part of your riding.

GENERAL ADVICE

Motorway riding

COPPS still applies but you need to plan much further ahead because you tend to travel at higher speeds.

- Try to anticipate the actions of other road users early, eg, a vehicle's brake lights come on four vehicles ahead. Use acceleration sense to reduce speed rather than leaving it too late. Avoid having to use your brakes, which may slow the traffic flow. Remember that the slip 'roads' are acceleration and deceleration lanes and use them properly.
- Know The Highway Code.
- Keep your machine clean, that way you'll see if it needs maintenance.
- Conspicuity. Try not to rely on being seen, always ride defensively. Having your lights on will certainly improve the chances of being seen but also can cause other road users to misjudge your speed and distance. Use them wisely and certainly do not use your high beam during the day.
- Practise and get the techniques right. They are designed to be used at high and low speeds.
- Remember, you will get far more satisfaction and respect from other bikers by doing it right than by going too fast, making a mistake and looking like an idiot.
- Movement will be seen by the human eye more than anything else. Always change position slightly when approaching a hazard.

Which advanced course?

This introduction has been written to give you an insight into becoming an advanced rider. There are many advantages to completing a professionally run, practical, advanced riding course, and it is the best way to learn. When deciding which training scheme to choose, bear in mind the following:

- What qualifications do they hold?
- How long have they been riding?
- What are the aims of the course?

Avoid any training that is all about speed, unless it is conducted off the public roads. If in doubt, contact your local police motorcycle unit. After all, these riders had to pass the toughest course in the world.

Above all, enjoy biking and stay safe!

Observe, plan,
anticipate, enjoy.

www.honda.co.uk

If you don't have wings, you'll never fly.

Get out on manoeuvres.

There's only one place to really improve your riding skills and that's out on the road. Which is exactly where one of our Honda Motorcycle Training Team instructors will be taking you when you sign up for the Motorcycle Appreciation Course. MAC courses are open to any level of rider with a bike of 500cc or more. There are also preferential fees for HUKRC members.

- Over 70 instructors each with a minimum of a Class 1 Police Advanced Motorcycle Riding Certificate.
- An instructor to rider ratio that is never more than one to two.
- A programme tailored to your needs, no matter which area of your riding you want to improve.
- Up to 16 hours of riding and on-the-road instruction over two full days.
- A sophisticated radio communication system to keep you in constant contact with your instructor when you're on the road.
- No need for special clothing or equipment. All you need is your usual safety gear with wet weather clothing recommended.
- Discounts on selected insurance policies when you sign up for a MAC course.

Ride smarter, feel safer and, above all, enjoy more. That's what our award winning Motorcycle Appreciation Course is all about. Letting you get the most out of biking you possibly can. Whether you're starting out or just need to sharpen your skills, MAC has some of the most highly qualified instructors in the world ready to help you fly.